D1259641

Ancient Peoples and Places

THE BYZANTINES

General Editor

DR. GLYN DANIEL

Ancient Peoples and Places

THE BYZANTINES

David Talbot Rice

95 PHOTOGRAPHS
25 LINE DRAWINGS
AND 5 MAPS

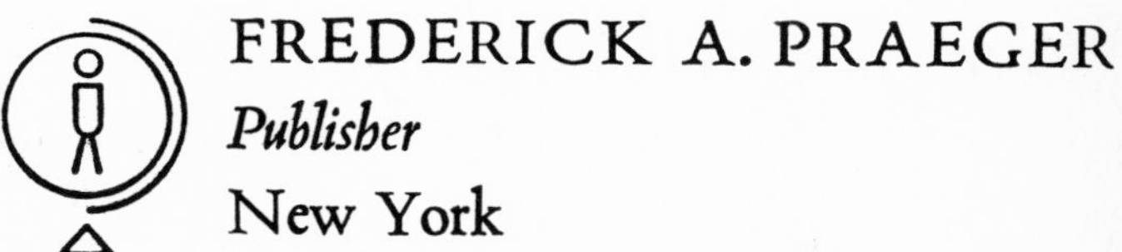

FREDERICK A. PRAEGER
Publisher
New York

THIS IS VOLUME TWENTY-SEVEN IN THE SERIES
Ancient Peoples and Places
GENERAL EDITOR: DR. GLYN DANIEL

BOOKS THAT MATTER *Published in the United States of America
in 1962 by Frederick A. Praeger, Inc.
Publisher, 64 University Place
New York 3, N.Y.*

Library of Congress Catalog Card Number: 62-15123

*Printed in Great Britain by Hazell Watson & Viney Ltd.
Aylesbury and Slough*

CONTENTS

ILLUSTRATIONS

FIGURES

To the memory of
Stanley Casson and Robert Byron,
with whom I first explored
Byzantium

Preface

THE TEXT CONTAINS no footnotes and only a very few books are mentioned in the bibliography, for it seemed unreasonable to overload what is essentially a general work with overmuch detail. I would, however, like to acknowledge here my great indebtedness to the numerous scholars whose books I have read during many years, and in particular to cite the names of Norman Baynes, George Ostrogorsky and Sir Steven Runciman. My very special thanks are also due to Mr P. D. Whitting, G.M., who organised the taking of photographs of coins in his own collection for Plate 59, and who was kind enough to provide the notes on the coins. I am indebted to Sir Basil Blackwell for permission to use a map in G. Ostrogorsky, *History of the Byzantine State,* for Figure 5. I would also like to thank my wife for valuable comments on the text and for the ideas she inspired during the many years of travel and research that we have undertaken together.

D. T. R.

Introduction

THE HISTORY of the Byzantine empire began with the foundation of Constantinople in 330 and ended when the last emperor died in the defence of the city before the Turkish onslaught of 1453. Byzantine culture, however, can hardly be confined within these limits, for though a change in outlook came about as a result of the adoption of Christianity as the official religion of the state in 313, it was not really until the age of Justinian (527–565) that the new approach was truly matured, and though the empire ended in 1453, Byzantine art and thought lived on in the Balkans and in Greece for many centuries, while Russia, as an independent Christian state, was an even more important heir. The heritage of Byzantium cannot however be dealt with here, and our story must end with the mid-fifteenth century. It may begin, for the sake of convenience, about the year 500, when the changes which were to reach fruition under Justinian had already been set in train.

The area that concerns us is similarly hard to define, for it varied from an empire which at the time of Justinian extended from Spain in the west to the Mesopotamian desert in the east and from the line of the Danube and Black Sea in the north to the coastal fringe of Mediterranean Africa in the south, to an area which, under the last of the Palaeologues, comprised little more than the city of Constantinople and some small territories in the Peloponnese. In spite of this, however, a region where Byzantine culture was firmly established throughout this age can be circumscribed; it comprised the whole of Asia Minor and Greece, the western Balkans, and parts of Sicily and south Italy; it was there that the main developments took place and it is with that area that we must be in the main concerned in spite of numerous ramifications elsewhere.

It is thus the central area and the period from around 500 till 1453 that will be discussed in these pages. More than that would be impossible in a book of this size. But if we can succeed in defining what it was that constituted the essentials of Byzantine culture and show that the history of the Byzantine world was not one of sterile monotony, still less of prolonged decay, as our forefathers supposed, our task will have been fulfilled.

CHAPTER I

The People

I have seen old ships sail like swans asleep
Beyond the village which men still call Tyre
With leaden age o'ercharged, dipping deep
For Famagusta and the hidden scene
That rings black Cyprus with a lake of fire.

J. E. FLECKER

WHO WERE THE BYZANTINES? Apart from giving the obvious answer that they were the inhabitants of the East Roman or Byzantine Empire, this is no very easy question to answer. The Byzantine empire was hardly an entity distinct from the Roman till the ninth century, and its inhabitants never constituted a definite ethnic group, like the Celts; they never formed a close cultural unit, like the Scythians; nor were their art and their influence confined to a limited area and period, as were those of the Etruscans. The term connotes rather a phase of civilisation, a way of life, developed to the full in a single centre, Constantinople, though the city dominated a wide cultural sphere over a period of some eleven hundred years – from 330 to 1453 to be exact. At one time, in the fifth and sixth centuries, nearly all the great cities of Christendom – Alexandria, Antioch and Jerusalem, Ephesus, Salonica and Athens, Ravenna, Milan and even Rome herself – were within this sphere and boasted an art and culture which were broadly Byzantine. At another, owing to the rise of Islam and the loss of control in the west, the extent of the empire was reduced to include only Asia Minor, the Balkans, Greece and southern Italy, though the Byzantine character of the culture was intensified. Finally, after the twelfth century, the emperor was often little more than a puppet under Turkish control, though the culture flourished and the Orthodox faith had achieved a unity and strength of purpose perhaps never equalled at an earlier date.

Needless to say the peoples who formed the population of this state in the days of its greatest glory were of extremely diverse racial stock. In early days the emperors and their immediate entourage were Romans and spoke Latin, though many of them had in their veins the blood of peoples whom the Romans had conquered in Gaul, Spain, Syria or North Africa. But with the move of the capital to Constantinople, Greeks began to play a more important role, and by the end of the sixth century Latin had almost entirely given place to Greek as the universal language of the Empire, and men who were Greeks in outlook as well as in speech occupied most of the more important governmental posts both in the capital and elsewhere. Later new dynasties were founded by men born and brought up in Macedonia, the Peloponnese, Asia Minor, or even Armenia, while the leading government officials were drawn from all over the empire and at times even from places outside it.

But from wherever they came and whatever their racial origins, the people, rich and poor alike, were none the less Byzantines, just as the citizens of the U.S.A. today somehow form a cultural unity, in spite of the immense diversity of racial elements that go to make up the north American population. Though Constantinople was the hub of the Byzantine world, the life that was lived in the various cities and towns of the Empire was Byzantine too. Similarly the army was in the main a Byzantine army, except towards the end, when mercenaries from as far afield as the Anglo-Saxon world and Scandinavia were employed as independent units which managed to retain their national identity, surviving in much the same way as the Swiss guard at the Vatican survives as an independent non-Italian unity in Italy at the present time.

Though the term Byzantine thus implies a way of life rather

than a racial unit, it is nevertheless important to examine the racial basis of the population of the main parts of the empire, that is to say, Constantinople and its hinterland, Greece, Asia Minor and the eastern Balkans. Other areas, Italy itself, Syria, Palestine, and lands like Armenia or Bulgaria, though they were sometimes within the bounds of the Empire, need not concern us in themselves, for they so clearly form units which were ethnically independent, however much they learnt and adopted from Byzantium proper. But they must concern us in so far as their peoples became at times Byzantine citizens and settled within the Byzantine state in the narrower sense of the term. This was especially the case with regard to the Armenians, who gave more than one Emperor to Byzantium, and who in the tenth century provided not only numerous officials but also a large percentage of the armed forces; it might almost be said that for a time Armenians operated a considerable part of the great machine of state. Runciman has compared their role to that of the Scots today.

Byzantium itself had always been a Greek city. It was founded by Byzas in 657 BC, but surprisingly enough, in spite of its magnificent geographic situation, it remained comparatively unimportant till Constantine chose it as the site for his new capital in AD 324 – it was refounded as Constantinople in 330. Its inhabitants, like those of the other Hellenistic cities of the coastal fringe – Priene, Pergamon, Miletus and so on – were Greeks; they spoke the Greek tongue and were racially members of the so-called Mediterranean group, to which the inhabitants of the whole Aegean area at this time in the main belonged. The influx of Romans who came with Constantine and his followers cannot numerically have been very considerable, and they were soon completely assimilated. *Fig. 1*

The same must have been true of the cities of the coastlands which had played a part in Greek history since very early times. Only when the plateau of Anatolia was ascended did the situation change, for the Greeks had never fully colonised this area, and the Romans had controlled it without being in any way assimilated. Such evidence as is available suggests that the population had altered but little since the days when the Hittite and allied rulers vied with one another for supremacy. Skulls that have been excavated show that the people of the uplands were even then mainly of the Armenoid racial type, their heads being broad and flat at the back. Intermixture, coming as the result of conquest and of migration, had of course begun well before the Christian era, especially in the more accessible regions, and we know from excavations that most of the ancient cities were continually being destroyed and re-founded. In many cases the new inhabitants brought with them a new culture and the supposition may be hazarded that they were often also members of a distinct ethnic group. Yet the old Armenoids survived, for their racial characteristics seem throughout to have been of a very dominant type.

The process of intermixture continued throughout Byzantine times. Land was offered for settlement as a reward for military service, and peoples were frequently moved from one area to another on a wide scale. At the time of Phocas (602–610), for example, there were as many as 60,000 military settlers in Asia Minor, and these people no doubt in the course of time intermarried with the local population. In 658 Constans II arranged a mass transportation of Slavs to Asia Minor and this was repeated in 689; in 747 prisoners from Syria and Armenia were settled in Thrace. In the twelfth century Serbians, Petchenegs and Hungarians were established in Asia Minor by John and Manuel Comnenus, and all through the middle period there were similar resettlements for religious reasons, members of heretical communities being transported to other regions in order to break them up.

The presence of Armenoid types in Anatolia today – some authorities put them as high as 75 per cent of the country's population – shows however that the racial changes cannot have been very wide-sweeping, and it is safe to conclude that the population of the uplands of Asia Minor cannot in Byzantine times have been very different from what it is at present. It was from there that the Byzantines drew their best troops and the excellence of the Turkish soldier today reflects no doubt the same racial heritage that distinguished the Byzantine army. It is also worthy of note that it was in these regions that the various Christian heresies had their strongest hold; this again attests to the determination, conservatism and obstinacy of the inhabitants of the area. They constituted the solid backbone of the state, an admirable counterpart to the volatile Greeks of the coastlands.

Here the population was probably much more mixed. According to some authorities the Phrygians, who occupied the plateau area to the east of the Sea of Marmara, had come from the west, and they were probably forced further eastwards by invasions from Thrace. Certainly there was a considerable introduction of peoples from Macedonia into western Asia Minor during the Hellenistic age, though they tended to keep aloof from the native population, retaining their own way of life and religion and their own social customs. Later still, in the eighth century AD, a few Slavs were forcibly settled, especially in Bithynia, but they were eventually absorbed and cannot ever have exercised a role of much importance. In 802 Nicephorus Phocas adopted the policy of granting land as a reward for service to sailors as well as to soldiers; such land was of course in the coastal regions. But these settlements can hardly have affected the population as a whole, and just as the inhabitants of the uplands were in the main Anatolians of Armenoid extraction, so those on the coastal fringes remained Greeks, stemming from the Mediterranean racial group.

The Balkan area presents a more complicated problem, for there migrations during the Byzantine era exercised a far more profound and lasting effect than in Asia Minor or on the coastal fringe. Indeed the Balkans were, racially speaking, an unstable area throughout the whole of the period with which we are dealing. In Roman times the population had to no small degree been affected by the Roman habit of repopulating sparsely inhabited or insecure areas with people brought from far afield. Thus when Trajan annexed Dacia in AD 107, colonists were imported from elsewhere in the Roman world, including some from Palmyra, while large numbers of Visigoths were settled to the south of the Danube in the time of Theodosius I (*c.* 390). But more important were the continued incursions south of the Danube by barbarian or semi-barbarian tribes, which began before the Christian era and continued till the ninth or tenth century, most of the newcomers arriving from the north or east, driven forward to south and west by the pressure of further bodies of migrants behind them. Huns were succeeded by Vandals, Vandals by Goths and Ostrogoths, Ostrogoths by Slavs, and Slavs by Petchenegs, and though the main effect of these migrations was exercised on Italy and Gaul, the northern Balkans was still in a permanent state of flux till the arrival of the Bulgars about 680 produced a well-organised and more or less stable element in the area we now know as Bulgaria. The Bulgars, whose culture was initially related to that of Persia, learnt from the Byzantines at an early stage, and though they were later to become one of the most formidable political rivals of Byzantium, they also became one of her most influential heirs in the spheres of thought, religion and art.

The movement of the Slavs was in the main southward, through what is today Yugoslavia, towards Salonica. It was most intense in the sixth century, when Tiberius II was forced to leave the frontier open owing to a greater menace on his eastern territory. The Slavs did not greatly affect the population of Thrace, which retained its old basic character in the main, though Leo III settled people from the eastern frontier there in the first half of the eighth century to constitute a bastion on which he could rely. Nor was the population of Greece as much changed by Slav incursions as has sometimes been supposed. The population of the countryside was driven southwards and indeed even overseas, so that there was an increase of Greeks in Sicily at the time and the Slavs even penetrated into the Peloponnese. But urban centres remained in the main unaffected and elsewhere the newcomers appear to have been rapidly assimilated. The most serious result of this invasion was probably the superficial one of a disruption of settled life and of road communication rather than a lasting one influencing profoundly the nature of the inhabitants.

The last wave of newcomers to the Balkans were the Albanians, a broad-headed people from the north who arrived in the thirteenth century. They never formed part of the Byzantine world properly speaking.

The cultured and ruling classes, the inhabitants of Constantinople itself and its surroundings and of the larger towns, were mainly of the Mediterranean race and were Greeks in outlook and in speech. In character and appearance they were no doubt easily distinguishable from the poorer classes who lived on the uplands of Asia Minor. They were however not so very different from the inhabitants of eastern Europe, excluding the Slavs. Like the Greeks of today, they were argumentative, excitable, vivacious. They loved discussion, and they got worked up over problems of government or belief; there were frequent minor revolutions, and it was impossible for anybody in authority to sit on his heels. Life for them was full of changes, and existence must have been anything but dull; the picture of a prolonged, slow decay that Gibbon presents is essentially out of keeping with their character and with the evidence of their art. There was much change, and constant variation, and a good deal of it was for the better, not for the worse.

Throughout the empire there was a leavening of peoples of

other types and other origins, settlers who often retained their own national characteristics and identity. Most important of these were the Jews, but their numbers after the seventh century can never have been very considerable. Other peoples, like the Arabs and Armenians, intermarried more frequently, and even if they did not greatly affect the ethnic scene, they must have been responsible for the introduction of new ideas and the assimilation of new customs. Gypsies were quite numerous in the Empire from the eleventh century onwards. But it was the Greek element, with all the faults, but with all the brilliant advantages, of that people, that played the major role in history and culture from round about the middle of the sixth century, and it is as one of the chapters in the long story of Greek culture and Greek thought that Byzantium must really be studied.

CHAPTER II

The Place

How is it that in the kingdoms of Persia, which are such near neighbours of ours, there are folk so unruly and contentious that they are forever killing one another, whereas among us, who are all but one with them, there is hardly an instance of provocation or brawling? The sages answered that it was due to a difference in the soil. So the King thereupon sent to Persia, and in particular to Isfahan aforementioned, whose inhabitants outdid the rest in every sort of villainy. There, on the advice of his sages, he had seven ships loaded with earth brought to his own kingdom. This earth he ordered to be spread out like pitch over the floors of certain rooms and then covered with carpets, so that those who entered should not be dirtied by the soft surface. Then a banquet was served in these rooms, at which the guests had no sooner partaken of food than one began to round on another with opprobrious words and actions that soon led to blows. So the King agreed that the cause did indeed lie in the soil.

The Travels of Marco Polo

THOUGH THE FRONTIERS of the Empire varied very considerably, the area that concerns us as the 'Byzantine world' can nevertheless be fairly exactly defined. To the north the Black Sea and the line of the Danube constituted a clearly marked frontier, beyond which Byzantine hegemony never actually extended, though at times political and commercial relations were established across it. To the west the mountains on the eastern shore of the Adriatic formed a natural barrier, which from the point of view of hampering cultural contacts was more effective than that of the sea to the west of them. To the south-east and east, even if Syria and Palestine were at first important parts of the empire, the mountains that today separate Turkey from Syria, Mesopotamia and Persia marked the frontier throughout the greater part of the age with which we are concerned as clearly as they mark today the border between the Turkish and the Arab and Persian lands. To the north-

Fig. 1

Fig. 1. The Byzantine World

R. Dniepr
Cherson
GEORGIA
ARMENIA
Kars
Ani
Trebizond
Samsun
Amasia
Constantinople
Chalcedon
Manzikert
Nicomedia
mara
Nicaea
Ankara
L. Van
zicus
BITHYNIA
Eskishehir
Diyarbekr
amon
PHRYGIA
MESOPOTAMIA
Myriokephalum
yrna
hesos
Konia
CILICIA
Taurus Mts
riene
Tiletus
ISAURIA
Side
Aleppo
Antioch
SYRIA
CYPRUS
Jerusalem
Alexandria
HAS

east again the separation between the Byzantine world on the one hand and Georgia and Armenia on the other was always fairly definite. Even if Armenia at times came under Byzantine rule, these countries were just as much a part of the Caucasian world as the so-called 'Little Armenia' in Cilicia, which was important in the twelfth century, was always a part of the Byzantine world.

NATURE OF BYZANTINE CULTURE

The geographical limits as thus defined give a clear indication of all that the word Byzantine stands for. Just as the empire was located at the eastern end of the Mediterranean, in an Hellenistic area, between the worlds of Rome and the east, so the culture of the empire was influenced from all these sources. Writers have tended to take up the cudgels stressing the influence of one area rather than another, and a very great deal has been written on the subject. But in truth neither the legacy of Rome, nor that of the east, nor, indeed, even that of the Hellenistic world, was alone responsible for the way in which Byzantine culture developed. Byzantium was both a 'thought-world' and a geographical area that was betwixt and between, owing a debt to west, east and centre alike, till the nature and degree of the debts became eclipsed beneath the new individuality that grew up as hall-mark of all that was Byzantine.

Constantinople was an ideal site for the capital of a state which owed this triple allegiance to geography. The city stands on the very borders of Europe and Asia, and Thrace on the one hand and western Asia Minor on the other constituted throughout the Empire's hey-day the most vital parts of its territory. But though Asia Minor is a part of the Asian continent, it is really neither geographically nor racially an integral part of Asia, while the eastern Balkans are equally hardly a part of Europe. They belong rather to that no-man's-land between the continents which is constituted by Russia to the north and Greece to the south; for there is and always has been a certain Asiatic element in the culture of European Russia, and Greece, though technically a part of Europe, seems somehow to lie apart, if not actually divorced from that continent, and to this day the inhabitants of Athens speak of 'going to Europe', rather than of going to France, to Italy, to Germany, or wherever it may be.

THE WORLD OF ORTHODOX CHRISTEN-DOM

Since the end of the Byzantine empire – indeed, since a date some three centuries before its actual collapse in 1453 – the force that has bound this no-man's-land between the continents into something of a unity has been the nature of its faith, Orthodox Christianity. Moscow looked upon itself in the fifteenth century as the new Constantinople, the third Rome; Greece today considers herself the heir of Byzantium just as much as the heir of the classical city states. Political ideology now disassociates her from Russia; the deep separation between Christianity and Islam, and old historical antipathies, alienate her from Turkey; differences of language and a certain degree of apprehension make difficult any close attachment between her and the Balkan Slavs. Yet, rising above all these differences, there is a basic bond, a similarity of thought and outlook, which goes back to the days of Byzantium and stands as one of the greatest legacies which that state left to the future.

It is not this larger area of Orthodox Christendom that concerns us here, so much as the more limited, though none the less distinctive region of the Byzantine empire as it was constituted in the days of Basil II in the tenth century. And to this empire, welded into one by great rulers and a centralised government, the key was the capital, Constantinople. *Fig. 4*

CONSTAN-TINOPLE AS EASTERN CAPITAL

The idea of transferring the capital from Rome to the east was not new: Nicomedia and Salonica had both been considered, but as we look back today there can be no disputing the wisdom of Constantine's choice. First the city was ideally placed with regard to trade, for it not only dominated the great sea route from north to south, which linked the civilised world of the Mediterranean with the rich natural resources of Russia, but also stood at the point where the land routes of Asia Minor and those across eastern Europe encountered the narrowest sea-crossing. Second, with the Sea of Marmara to the south and the Golden Horn to the north, it was admirably placed from the point of view of defence; the very fact that every other city at one time or another succumbed to attack or was sacked while Constantinople withstood every siege till the end affords tangible proof of this. It was defended along the water line by sea *Fig. 2* Plates 1, 2 walls and on the one landward front Constantine built a single straight wall from the Golden Horn to the Marmara; this was replaced by a parallel but stronger wall a mile or so further to the west in the time of Theodosius II in order to give more space in the town. That wall, some six kilometres long, survives to this day, testimony alike to the excellence of its construction and to the wisdom of the man who selected the city for his capital.

And finally, not only was Constantinople admirably sited as a fortress and a trading centre; even more important, it was ideally situated to cope with the problems of imperial defence. In Constantine's day there were two main enemies, the Persians to the east and the barbarian tribes beyond the Danube to the north, and from no other place could action on the two fronts be so satisfactorily co-ordinated. And later, when the west also became a source of danger and the emperors had to cope time and again with simultaneous threats from the Arab world and from Italy, the prophetic genius of Constantine's choice was amply justified. Only at the end, when the city had become a head without a body, was the situation altered. Then a small town like Nicaea or Mistra might have flourished where Constantinople foundered.

Constantinople had an excellent climate, never too hot and seldom very cold. The surrounding area furnished admirable agricultural and horticultural possibilities and the sea provided fish; fish, vegetables and bread seem to have made up the staple

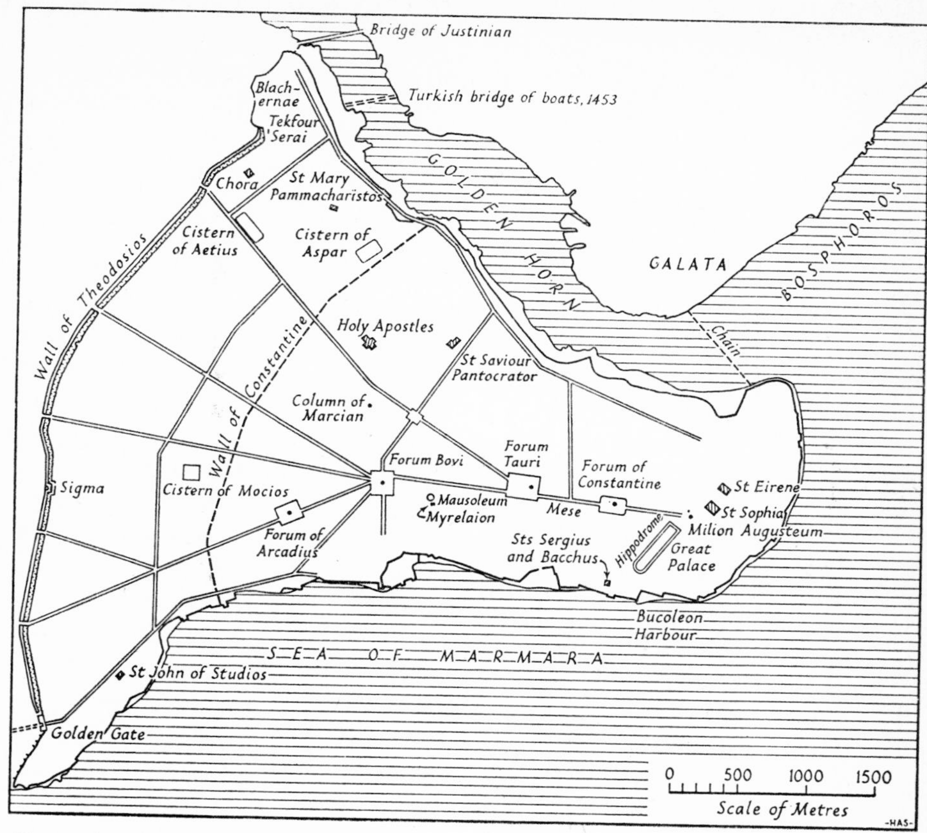

Fig. 2. Plan of Constantinople

diet of most of the population through the whole period of Byzantine history. Indeed, in respect of fresh foods the city was almost entirely self-sufficing and only the grain had to be imported. Inside the area confined by its walls, a series of small hills afforded variety and permitted experiments of lay-out and at the same time left adequate space for gardens and water storage, both equally essential for life, especially at a time of siege. The water was led into the town by a series of aqueducts Plate 3 running partly above and partly below ground, but in case these were cut or the supply otherwise interrupted a great mass of cisterns was constructed, some open, the size of small lakes, others underground, with roofs supported on a mass of columns Plates 5, 7 and arches. Forty or so covered cisterns survive to this day, some of them still full of water; one of the most impressive is known by the Turks as The Cistern of a Thousand and one Columns, and another, still full of water, as the Underground Palace. These, and many of the others too, are architectural structures of great beauty and distinction. With the aid of the rainfall they would have served to support the population through the longest siege and the aqueducts that led into the town were a luxury to provide a lavish and fresh supply of water, rather than a real necessity.

There was a similarly elaborate drainage system, and pipes of the Byzantine period, fitting one into the other with socketed joints, are encountered whenever an excavation is made. They are connected with larger conduits of brick with vaulted tops, Plate 6 many of them high enough to walk along. Today it is not always easy to say which of them were originally conduits for fresh water, and which drains leading eventually to the sea. But their number serves to establish the complicated nature of the Byzantine water and drainage system.

There was one main street, the Mese, which led from the principal Plate 4 entrance through the land walls, the Golden Gate, to the place of the Augusteum, which lay between Haghia Sophia and the Great Palace of the Emperors. This street passed through a number of fora in which stood columns decorated with sculptures or other prominent monuments. The columns of Arcadius, Theodosius, Marcian and Constantine were the most important of them, and the two latter still stand. A great triumphal arch supported on columns with a curious 'peacock's Plate 8 feather' decoration marked the entrance to the Forum of Theodosius; its remains were discovered in 1927 and have recently been fully unearthed in the process of street widening. The same emperor set up an obelisk from Egypt upon a sculptured base in the Hippodrome. Plate 9

Apart from the various fora, the Mese must have been an impressive thoroughfare, for it was wide, straight and well paved, and had arcades on either side, in any case near the centre of the town. From the Forum of Theodosius a branch led past the church of the Holy Apostles to the Blachernae Palace and the walls near the Golden Horn, and similar, but smaller, streets led to the other gates in the land walls. Many of these streets were apparently also adorned with monuments. The side streets of the Byzantine capital were, on the other hand, narrow and winding. Transport was by mule or by porters and the normal means of progress was on foot. In fact, the aspect of the streets must have been very similar to that predominating until a few decades ago, when motor cars began to supplant the old 'hamals' or porters and the donkeys and mules. The same was also true of the shopping quarters, for the trades centred in certain streets or areas, and there were bazaars which must have been very like those that survive to this day.

It is not easy to arrive at any very exact estimate of the size of the population, except perhaps just after plagues in 746 and 747, when it was probably around 500,000. It can hardly ever have dropped below this figure except in the fifteenth century; at times it may well have exceeded it quite considerably, and the figure of a million has been suggested for the days of greatest prosperity. Deaths at a rate of 10,000 per day are recorded after the plagues of 541 and 543, but this figure is surely an exaggeration. In a city which covers an area of some twenty square kilometres there need never, even when the population was at its greatest extent, have been need for overcrowding.

OTHER CITIES OF THE EMPIRE

For more than a thousand years, with one brief interval from 1204 to 1261, Constantinople was the capital of the Byzantine world and the nucleus of Byzantine civilisation; for more than half that period its importance eclipsed that of all the other cities of the empire put together. Indeed except for Antioch and Alexandria in early times and Salonica both then and at a later date, it is surprising what an insignificant role most of the other cities of the empire seem to have played. They are but seldom mentioned in the texts and there is reason to believe that after the seventh century they mostly declined in size and importance even if they stood in regions which were wholly untouched by the advance of Islam. In any case most of them ceased to mint their own bronze coins at this time, though they had done so throughout the Roman and earlier Byzantine periods. They survived as Bishoprics, so there can have been no great falling off in the numbers of their population even if they did lose all political significance. They probably became centres of large rural communities rather than urban cities in their own right, and many of the inhabitants appear to have been employed in the neighbouring countryside rather than in the cities themselves. Their power and importance was further reduced by the introduction of the *theme* system by Heraclius, as a result of which the countryside was divided into a series of military provinces. But it would be wrong to think that there were no cities. Benjamin of Tudela in the twelfth century mentions one at practically every stopping place on his journey, whether he was travelling along the coast by sea or overland. It was, rather, the concentration of all political and major trading activities in Constantinople that was responsible for our lack of information about the towns, and even if the records are scanty, the great wealth of the state, especially in the ninth, tenth and eleventh centuries, attests a prosperity which must have been universal.

Fig. 5

Repercussions of political events at the capital – the assassination of an emperor, disputes with the patriarch, the revolt of a legion – can have penetrated but slowly to the provincial cities, still more slowly to the countryside. Day-to-day life was essentially local, and its course probably depended far more on the demands and character of the individual tax collector than on events in a wider sphere, which have left their mark on history. Nor can the devastations wrought by invading armies have been very lasting, for the path of their progress must have been restricted. The mountains and valleys must indeed have been at once a boon and an overriding problem to the tactical commanders, and a garrison may well have held out in a hill-top castle long after the surrounding country had fallen.

NATURE OF ASIA MINOR

The build of the great land mass of Asia Minor is distinctive. The boundary to the north is clearly defined by the Black Sea, that to the south almost equally so by the mountains that separate the plateau from the lowland plains of Syria and Iraq. To the east the mountains rise to form a barrier even more formidable than the Alps and these mountains have, throughout history, constituted a clearly marked border between Asia Minor on the one hand and on the other cultured Persia to the south and the wild barbarian world of the steppes to the north. To the west the barrier is less well defined, for the broken coast fades more or less imperceptibly into the islands and these in turn seem to afford a continuous link across the sea with the mainland of Greece. The physical characteristics of the land thus bear close relation to history; in Byzantine times the boundary between what is today Greece and what is today Turkey was never an actual one, whereas the eastern frontier was always a defensive line.

The western coastal fringe of Asia Minor and the numerous valleys leading inland from it are rich and fruitful. From very early times a large population was centred in this area, life was easy and the climate favourable. It was there that the great cities of Hellenistic times – Pergamon, Priene, Ephesus, Miletus and the rest – were situated, and there that much that was good in Greek culture had had its origin. The region remained vital and creative throughout Byzantine history.

The coastal fringe of the Black Sea is less clement. Firstly, over much of its length it is narrow, the mountains bordering the central plateau rising up suddenly and steeply within a few hundred yards of the coast, while the valleys that penetrate them are steep and precipitous and the rivers a source of danger at flood time rather than a means of communication. But the groves of nuts on the lower slopes and the forests on the higher ones must always have been important, while the coastal ports as a whole offered ready communication on the one hand across the sea with Constantinople or with the rich Greek trading colonies of the Crimea and south Russia, and on the other by the mountain passes with the plateau to the south. At the eastern end of the Black Sea the trade routes extended much further inland, to Armenia, Persia and thence to Central Asia and the Far East, and they were always important, especially after the seventh century, when the advances of Islam cut those across Syria and Mesopotamia.

AGRICULTURE

The central plateau of Asia Minor, which in area is far greater than that of the coastal fringes, is in climate a good deal less clement. High in altitude, it is cold in winter and hot in summer, with a rather thin soil capable of producing only modest crops without elaborate terracing and irrigation, and there is no evidence to suggest that much was done in this way in Byzantine times. There are rich lowlands, especially in the west and south-west, and these constituted important grain-producing areas in the Byzantine economy. It was there, around Amasia and Ancyra (Ankara) to the north, around Iconium (Konia) in the centre, and in Cilicia in the south, that the largest cities existed. To the east, as the land rose in a series of progressively severer ranges until the mountains of the anti-Caucasus were reached, the cities became fewer and the villages smaller, able to produce enough scanty crops to feed their own inhabitants, but leaving little surplus. Their flocks of sheep and goats were on the other hand extensive and the empire must have depended on them to a considerable degree.

It was also primarily in the mountains that the mines were situated.

THE AEGEAN

The build of most of the Islands of the Aegean repeats that of Asia Minor on a smaller scale. True, there is not necessarily the same west to east incline, but the interiors are usually mountainous and rugged, the population and cultivation being mainly concentrated on the coasts. Their agricultural products served to support the inhabitants, but there was probably little to spare in the way of exports but for wine and meat. They cannot have contributed much to the imperial economy and, so far as we can learn from the records, they were even little relied on as a source of man-power for the army. Nor were troops from the mainland of Greece very numerous, though Thracians and others from the north were regularly recruited. Here again, the land-build of Greece was of a nature to restrict agricultural output, and the mountainous interior made communications far from easy. Only in the lands to the north, the coastal area from Salonica eastwards, and especially Thrace, did geographical conditions favour a life which was truly useful to the empire, namely a thoroughly prosperous agriculture and a large population which would provide a surplus for the army and for industry.

Even so, Thrace was never really as important as Asia Minor, and when the latter area began to fall away to the Seljuks in the twelfth century, the power and wealth of the whole empire began to decline also; without Asia Minor the Byzantine state could never have recovered fully, whatever might have been the outcome of events in eastern Europe. Possession of a prosperous Asia Minor was in fact essential to the well-being of the State. Its significance was fourfold: as a strategic area, dominating communications with the east, as a source of food, as a source of man-power, and because of its mines.

The strategic importance of Asia Minor is obvious when it

is remembered that until its extinction in 650 the principal enemy of the Byzantine state was Sasanian Persia, with which power there was a common frontier from Armenia in the north almost to the line of the Euphrates in the south, and that with the rise of Islam the whole of the lowland and the plateau, from Mediterranean to Caucasus, was under the control of a new, powerful and in the main antagonistic rule. Unless this lengthy frontier was constantly patrolled and strongly held it was a source of terrible weakness. Though the main defence was of a static character, a sort of territorial army being installed along the frontier, more mobile forces were also required, and these had to be moved and supplied.

THE ROAD SYSTEM

For this purpose a good system of roads was essential. The Byzantine roads more or less followed those of the Romans, though certain new routes were brought into operation as the Byzantine empire developed. The Roman system in Asia Minor was in the main on an east to west basis, connecting the great cities of the coastal fringe like Ephesus and Pergamon directly with the interior, whereas in Byzantine times greater stress was laid on roads running from north-west to east and south-east, so that they provided communications between the upland and the capital. The change was actually set in motion by Diocletian in favour of Nicomedia and little further development of his plans was necessary when Constantine moved the capital to Byzantium.

There were thus two main roads from Constantinople, both of which passed through Nicomedia, one running more or less parallel with the Black Sea coast to Amasia, the other running south-east to Dorylaeum (Eskişehir), and then branching either eastwards to Ancyra (Ankara) or southwards to Iconium (Konia). As time went on, the character of the roads was further altered, in that they became less and less the great military highways of an imperialist state and more and more the trade routes of an economic one. Short roads linking the hinterland with some port or a town with the countryside were thus developed in addition to the great military highways and routes of Roman times. The Roman occupation had been concentrated along the roads; the Byzantine was a civilisation of the whole country.

In Europe the change was less marked, for the continuation of the via Egnatia, running from Constantinople to Adrianople, Neapolis, Philippi and Salonica, always remained important and there was another great road to the north leading to Bulgaria. Other routes were mostly of a local character. In Greece of course there was a great deal of intercommunication by sea. But we know little. One of the outstanding needs of the archaeological study of this period is a fuller investigation of the Byzantine, as opposed to the Roman, road system.

COMMUNICATIONS BY SEA

In spite of the importance of the roads, it was perhaps the sea communications that were most essential, and they were equally vital both from the commercial and the strategic points of view. Not only was the Byzantine navy efficient; not only did improvements in rigging and navigational methods greatly facilitate communication; not only was there a great overseas trade to be coped with; even more, the geographical build of the Empire dictated that sea routes had an outstanding role to play. From the time of Justinian onwards they were developed, and even if the south Mediterranean sea trade passed to the Moslems in the seventh century, that in the north remained in Byzantine hands till the rise of the Italian trading cities – Amalfi, Pisa, Genoa, Venice – in the later twelfth century challenged Byzantine supremacy and brought about a new distribution of economic prosperity and political power.

Underwater archaeology, that promising new science, has already begun to give some idea of the nature and extent of this sea trade and in certain danger-spots, where wind was prone to sudden changes or difficult currents hindered navigation, considerable numbers of wrecks have been plotted. Some of the ships no doubt carried perishable cargoes, grain, spices, wine, even vegetables, and these of course have vanished, though the large amphorae that contained these things remain. But others were laden with things of a more permanent nature like pottery, roofing tiles or metal. One of the most interesting tasks that awaits the archaeologist and the student of economics is to be found in an extensive investigation of these wrecks; and it may prove to be fruitful to the art-historian too, for who knows what treasures were not carried by sea in addition to the necessities?

Without these sea communications the land areas would in many cases have been cut off from one another, and, more important, from the capital. It was to a great extent thanks to them that the Byzantine state survived even after the defeat of Manzikert in 1071 and the resulting loss of so much of the vital area of Asia Minor to the Seljuks. Thus the sea played a role almost as vital as that of the land in Byzantine history, and, in any study of the geography of the area, just as much attention should be paid to it as to the role of the navy in a study of Byzantine political and economic history or to the influence of religious ideas in any study of Byzantine thought.

MINERALS

Fig. 3

Apart from its strategic importance and its role as the main centre of agriculture and chief source of man-power in the state, Asia Minor was also valuable for its mines. These had been worked in ancient times, and they no doubt continued in operation throughout the whole Byzantine period, though we do not know much about them except that mining was a state monopoly. The principal mines were either in the Pontic mountains, between Trebizond and Kars, or in the Taurus. Gold was found there, near the coast and in the Caucasus, but never, apparently, in very large quantities. Silver was mined in the Taurus, on the upper reaches of the Tigris, near Samsum and at Gumuşhane, near Trebizond, a name which in Turkish means House of Silver. Lead was found in many of the same places. Copper came from the Taurus, the Upper Tigris,

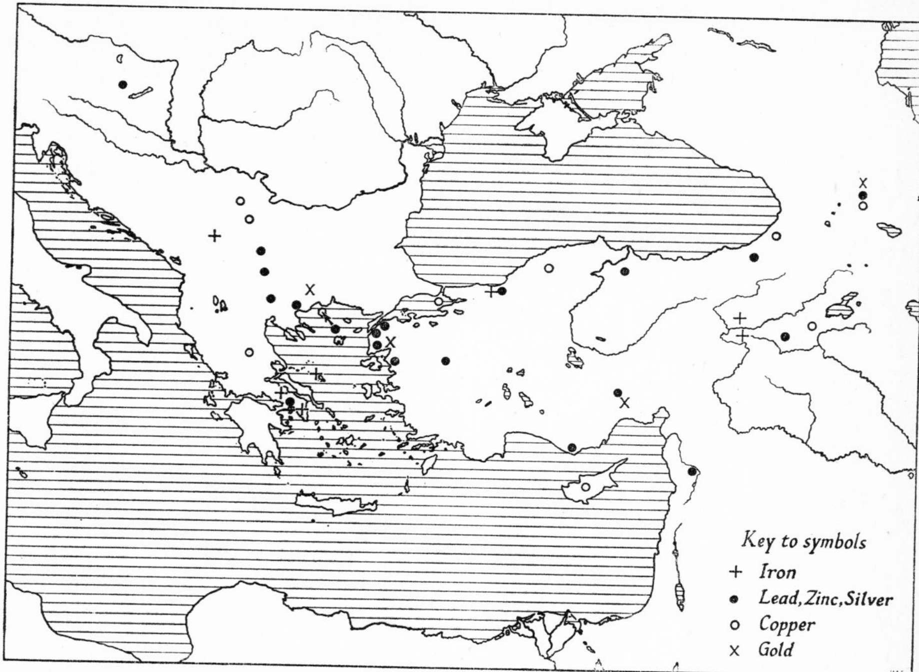

Fig. 3. Sources of minerals in the Byzantine World

Cyprus and the Trebizond region; the richest mines were probably those in the neighbourhood of Diyarbekr, though there were also smaller mines further to the west, notably on the Island of Halki (Heybeli Ada) near Constantinople, and in Thrace. Lead was also found in Macedonia. Iron was found in Greece, on the upper Tigris and in the Caucasus, but only in comparatively small quantities. Precious stones were also found sporadically in Asia Minor: lapis lazuli, for example, came from Nicomedia. Nevertheless a good deal had to be imported, and some at least of Byzantine metal probably came from overseas.

CHAPTER III

Their History

Rejoice, ye dead, where'er your spirits dwell,
Rejoice that yet on earth your fame is bright,
And that your names, remember'd day and night,
Live on the lips of those who loved you well.
Now ye are starry names
Behind the sun ye climb
To light the glooms of Time
With deathless flames.

ROBERT BRIDGES, *Odes*

THE STORY OF the external relationships of a state – its political history – does not always run in very close accord with the basic nature of its internal character – its cultural make-up. This is particularly true of Byzantium. There were undoubtedly periods of political expansion when the frontiers were extended and Byzantium stood in the forefront as a military power – under Justinian, Heraclius or Basil II – and these coincided with phases of great internal prosperity. But in the political sphere these periods of advance were the exception rather than the rule, and the title of Gibbon's great work *The Decline and Fall of the Roman Empire* is no doubt a just one in so far as the political, and more especially the military, history is concerned; indeed, as one reads of the intrigues, murders and schemings for power that colour so much of the background, one tends to be surprised that the empire lasted as long as it did. But the cultural history of Byzantium presents a very different picture. Even at the very end, when the empire had been reduced to the city of Constantinople and the little town of Mistra in the Peloponnese and when the Byzantine army had virtually ceased to exist, there dawned in these two places a renaissance of thought and art of great significance, while in the later eleventh and twelfth centuries, when affairs at home and on the frontiers were going from bad to worse, Byzantine art was exercising an influence abroad, not only in the Byzantinising areas of southern Italy and Venice but also in the rest of Italy, which was probably greater than at any other period; greater in any case even than in the tenth century when Byzantium politically speaking was at the height of its power.

FOUNDATION OF THE NEW ROME

Our story in some ways begins with the foundation of Constantinople as the New Rome in 330, for it was then that the new ideas that were to form the basis of the Byzantine state were born. It was the establishment of the Patriarchate there, in close association with the Emperor, that led eventually to the split between the two Churches, the Orthodox and the Latin. It was the concentration of government in the east that led to the adoption of a new outlook and to the establishment of what Baynes called a new 'thought-world'. The palace of the emperors on the slopes overlooking the Marmara, which was later to become the virtual hub of the civilised world, was begun by Constantine. The idea of a great wall linking the Golden Horn and the Marmara was first conceived by him, and it was he who began the first Haghia Sophia which was to become the centre of Orthodox Christendom. But the first two centuries of the new empire's life were really the prelude to, rather than a constituent part of, our period, even though many works of art were produced which were already Byzantine rather than Roman. The language of the court was still Latin, not Greek; the coinage can hardly be classed as Byzantine before the time of Anastasius I (491–518); the old patrician aristocracy was still powerful; there was still room for an emperor like Julian (361–363) to turn back to pagan gods; the old basilical form was still adhered to in church architecture; through much of the time there were still emperors in Italy and Italy's role in the development of art and thought was a separate and distinct one.

Ideas were certainly changing, but the age was still 'Early Christian' rather than Byzantine, and the eyes of the world were directed to the past as much as to the future.

JUSTINIAN

The year 500, however, marks a turning point. Independent emperors had ceased to rule in the west; by that time an art which was no longer Roman had begun to develop, and a new way of life and a new outlook had already been established. It was however as a result of the rule of a man of outstanding genius, Justinian (521–565), that the seal was firmly set on the new state, more particularly in the political sphere. It is hard to decide whether greatest credit should be ascribed to him for his insight as a builder and patron of art, for his work as the man who inspired a codification of the laws which has affected legislation to this day, or for his energy as a conqueror who extended the frontiers of the empire almost to their borders as at the hey-day of Roman imperialism. Or should one revere him most, perhaps, for his brilliant judgement in selecting the right men to serve him? Belisarius, the general who conquered Africa in 533; Narses, the eunuch, who brought Belisarius' campaigns in Italy to a successful conclusion around 555; Tribonian, to whom was entrusted the task of codifying the laws; Anthemius of Tralles, the foremost of the architects, 'not of that age only, but of all times', as a contemporary wrote, who built Haghia Sophia; or John of Cappadocia, to whom was entrusted the unenviable task of raising the funds to finance all these vast enterprises. Justinian has been described as the last of the Roman emperors; more truly he was the first of the Byzantines, for his aim was to assure the triumph of the new Christian state rather than to restore the Roman empire. He closed the pagan university at Athens in 529 and abolished many of the old offices, among them the Consulate in 541. And he, more than any other, was responsible for the centralisation of power and authority which was to become the hall-mark of the Byzantine state. From his day onwards the role of the capital

Fig. 4

became more and more important, while the provincial towns declined. He himself was at once controller of home affairs, commander-in-chief and head of the Church, as well as emperor in the conventional sense of the term.

The codified laws, and the renown of the cities and buildings he founded, have survived through the centuries to attest the glory of Justinian's reign. The empire faded almost overnight at his death. The Gothic tribes in north Italy were never really subdued in spite of Narses' victories; Spain was all lost by 572; the Slavs began to settle in the Balkans soon after the middle of the sixth century; and though Africa, Syria and Palestine were held for a time, they fell easily enough before the determined advance of Islam in the seventh century. In fact, though the prosperity of Justinian's reign left its lasting mark in the cultural and artistic spheres, the effects of his conquests were purely ephemeral and the empire was economically and politically the poorer rather than the richer as a result.

In the east, it is true, Justinian's successors made some progress; much of Armenia passed to Byzantium as the result of a treaty made with Persia in 570 by Maurice, but he was dethroned in 602, and the reign of Phocas, who was proclaimed emperor in his stead by the army, marked an era of almost continuous military disaster, which culminated in the capture of Jerusalem by the Sasanian Persians in 613. They even advanced on Constantinople a few years later, and at the same time the Avars attacked from the north. An overwhelming defeat seemed in sight, until an individual once more came to the fore in the person of the emperor Heraclius (610–641). Realising the weakness of the state he had on his accession instituted a series of reforms, which enabled him after three or four years to redeem the situation.

HERACLIUS

The essence of his reforms was the organisation of the countryside into a series of military provinces or *themes* as they were called. They were named after the regiments stationed in the

Fig. 5

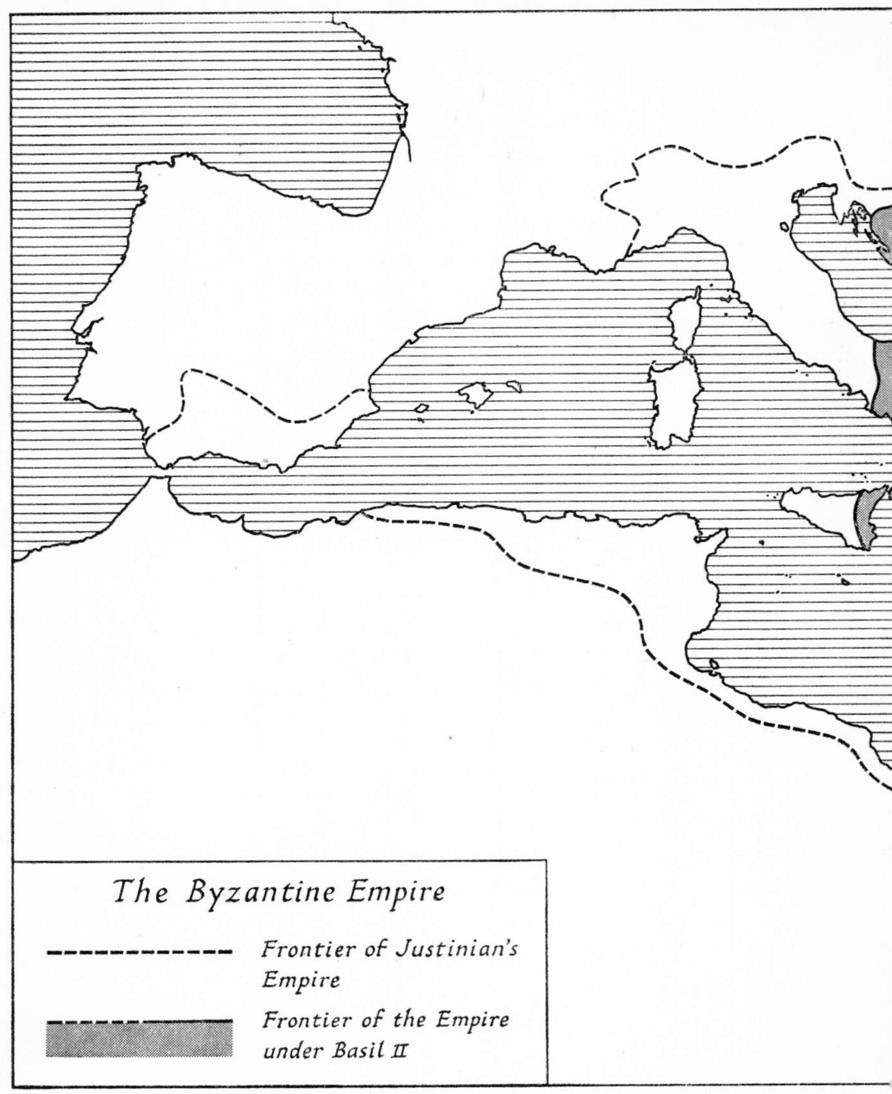

Fig. 4. The Byzantine Empire under Justinian and Basil II

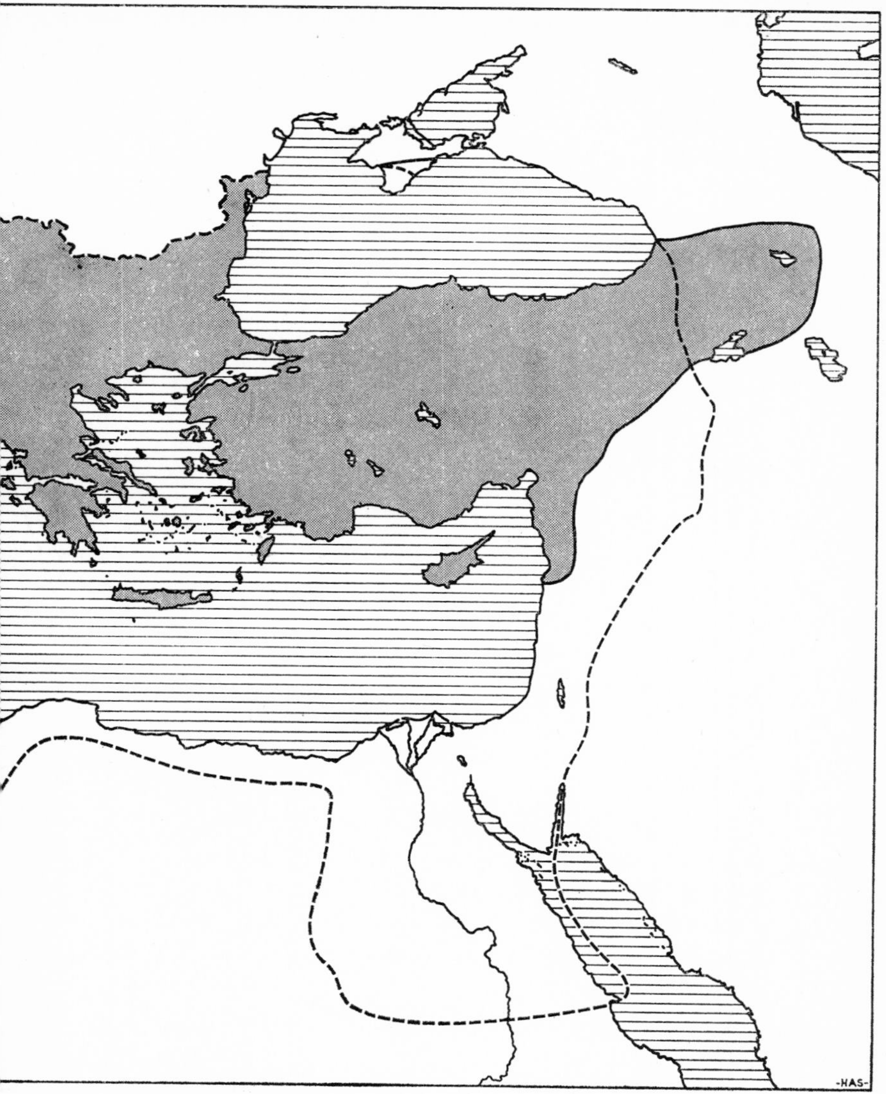
-HAS-

THE THEMES

area and took the place of the old and much larger provinces. Each was under the control of a *strategos* or general, with a proconsul under him to look after the civil administration. Asia Minor was first divided in this way and the Balkans soon after, making twenty-five *themes* in all; as time went on their number was considerably increased. At the same time troops were settled on the land, especially in the frontier regions, to form a sort of territorial force. The establishment of the *themes* was rather similar to a general proclamation of martial law. The military were put in control; each *strategos* was directly responsible to the emperor, and had at the same time to be ready to take quick action in his own area. Later the *strategoi* of the *themes* were to furnish not a few claimants to the throne. For the moment the system made for greater efficiency and greater flexibility.

Plate 59, *c*

With this new organisation established, Heraclius was able to conclude a peace with the Avars and to set out against Persia in 622, and in the following years a series of successful campaigns were conducted on the eastern frontier, especially in Armenia. But the pendulum could not be so easily swung in the opposite direction, and in 626 the Persians were again advancing on Constantinople. Byzantine naval power – and, as the Byzantines believed, the miraculous help of the Virgin – saved the day, and the next year Heraclius invaded Persia; in 628 the Persians capitulated and in 630 the True Cross, which they had captured in 613, was returned to Jerusalem. Only ten years were however to elapse before a new and more formidable enemy arose in the form of militant Islam, and by soon after 640 the whole of Syria, Palestine and Egypt had been lost, this time mostly for ever.

But if Heraclius' conquests were soon nullified, the system he had instituted survived, to form the basis of Byzantine government for the next five hundred years. This was no mean accomplishment in itself; its more immediate effect was to be seen in the fact that the Arabs, who carried all else before them, were unable to achieve any real success against the Byzantines. Advances were made in 663, again in 672, when Smyrna was captured, and again in 674, when the Arab fleet reached Constantinople, an event only made possible by the fact that the Caliph Moawiyah had realised that if he was to make headway at all, it was essential to build up his own naval power. But even so, thanks to some extent to the secret of Greek fire, the Byzantine forces were able to resist and in 678 the Arabs withdrew. With the menace from the east checked, the Byzantines were able to move against the Balkans. The Bulgarian kingdom had been recognised by Constantine IV (668–685), but in 688 an advance was made against the Slavs who were already settled in Illyria and had even begun to penetrate into Greece, pushed forward from the region of the Vistula and upper Dniepr by the migrations of Huns and other nomads behind them. From that time onward relationship with the Slavic peoples was to constitute one of the principal problems of Byzantine foreign policy; their contacts with Byzantium on the other hand were to give the Slavs their religion, their art, their culture and indeed the whole basis of their way of life.

Even if there were some military successes, the course of imperial history for the next twenty years was somewhat depressing. The autocratic rule of Constantine IV's successor, Justinian II, led to his deposition in 695; but after two brief and unimportant reigns he again claimed the throne in 705 with Bulgarian assistance. He died in 711, and his successor Philippicus was murdered by the army in 713. Anastasius II, a prominent civil servant, was crowned in his stead, but this displeased the army, who proclaimed Theodosius III emperor; he was at once deposed and followed Anastasius to a monastery, and Leo, *strategos* of the Anatolicon *theme*, became emperor in 717. It speaks well for the organisation of the state that after some twenty so disrupted years Leo was able to defeat the Arabs in their last attack against Constantinople, though it must be admitted that the pestilence and famine which broke out in their ranks probably played no small part in the destruction of their forces. Moreover, the emperor was able to gain the support of the Bulgars and the Khazars against them.

LEO III AND ICONOCLASM

With Leo III's reign (717–740) a more stable period set in. His first action was directed to governmental reforms, in an effort to stop judicial bribery, always rife in the Byzantine world; the *themes* were also to some extent reorganised. In this respect his rule was sound and effective. It was in the sphere of religion that it brought disharmony, for in 726 he enforced an edict against the representation of the divine or saintly form in art.

His first action – an attempt to move the famous icon of the Chalcopratia – was violently resisted at Constantinople; the western world rebelled, and a number of prelates and writers, with the Patriarch Germanus and the theologian John of Damascus foremost among them, took up a position against his proposed reforms. In 730 Leo resorted to force; Germanus was deposed, all opposition was suppressed with violence, and certain territories of the Pope in Sicily and Calabria were sequestered and transferred to the control of the Patriarch, for the Popes were always violently opposed to Iconoclasm.

Leo's Iconoclast policy was carried forward by his successor, Constantine V (740–775), who had already been crowned as co-emperor at the age of two, and in 754 he summoned a synod of the Church which gave general sanction to the tenets of Iconoclasm. His was a very complex character. On the one hand he was severe and brutal, pushing his Iconoclast beliefs to a degree equalled only by the worst terrors of the Inquisition. On the other he was a brilliant soldier, whose campaigns brought great glory to Byzantine history. He was victorious in Syria and Armenia; the Byzantine fleet won great battles in 747, and again in 763, and in 773 he was successful against the

Bulgars. Two years later he was killed in a further campaign against them.

Constantine was succeeded by Leo IV (775–780), a moderate, whose short reign was not very important, and he was followed by his son, Constantine VI; as he was only ten years old, his mother Irene, a remarkable personality who dominated affairs for the next twenty years, acted as regent. She favoured the icons and reversed the policy of her predecessors, appointing a new patriarch in the person of Tarasius and calling a council to rescind the decisions of the pro-Iconoclast synod of 754. It was broken up by soldiers, but met again at Nicaea in 787. The Iconoclasts were nevertheless still strong; they collected around Constantine and in 793 the religious disputes led to a period of civil war. But support was half-hearted; in 797 Constantine was blinded by his mother, who became sole ruler, the first woman to achieve this position. But her rule was not very successful. To secure popularity she reduced taxes, and this resulted in a disastrous financial crisis; she neglected the frontiers and was faced with attack from two sides, for Arab incursions had been taking place since 781 and in the Balkans the Byzantine forces were defeated by the Bulgars in 792. At the same time prestige in the west was falling as a result of the rise of the Carolingian Empire and events were brought to a head by the crowning at Rome in 800 of Charlemagne as emperor of the West, which was no doubt designed as a gesture by the Pope to indicate that he no longer owed allegiance to the Byzantine emperors. The idea of a single emperor was deep set, and this event marked more than anything else the split between Italy and Byzantium as well as that between the Latin and the Orthodox Churches. Charlemagne made an effort to achieve union – to his advantage – by sending an embassy to propose marriage to Irene, but she was deposed before it arrived and a court official, Nicephorus, was crowned in 802.

His first act was to stabilise the economy and to make new

grants of land for military service; an interesting feature of his reforms was that grants were made to sailors as well as soldiers. The situation in the Balkans was quickly consolidated; new *themes* were established there, and the Bulgarian leader Krum was defeated in 811. But the victorious Nicephorus was killed in battle almost immediately after, and a *coup d'état* brought Michael Rhangabe to the throne; the Balkan war flared up; the emperor was defeated by Krum in 813 and was at once deposed, to be succeeded by Leo V the Armenian (813–820). Like Leo III he was the *strategus* of the Anatolicon *theme* and an Iconoclast. The military disasters of the preceding years were attributed by him to a lack of zeal in prosecuting Iconoclast policy, and he called a synod in 815 which repudiated the anti-Iconoclast findings of the council of 787. As it happened the external situation did improve, even if not for Leo's reasons. Krum died suddenly in 813 and his successor Omurtag concluded a thirty years' truce, while in the east internal dissensions among the Abbasids put a stop to Arab incursions which had been more or less continuous since about 780. The Moslems did however capture Crete in 816 and Sicily in 827, as the Byzantine navy had been seriously neglected.

In 820 Leo was murdered by his old comrade in arms Michael II the Amorian, a rough soldier who took little interest in religious problems, though he suppressed an Iconodule rising led by one, Thomas. In 829 he was succeeded by his son Theophilus, a highly cultured and just ruler, but a convinced Iconoclast, who had been educated by one of the most able thinkers of the group, John the Grammarian. There was some persecution of the icon lovers from 832 to 836, but his reign really marked the end of the dispute. His military failures were attributed to his Iconoclast leanings, and soon after the accession of his successor Michael III in 820 the support for the movement began to wane, and in 843, under the regency of Theodora, the icons were restored. Once again affairs improved with a change of policy. The financial situation recovered, education was fostered and the frontiers were quiet.

Theodora's regency lasted till 856 when Michael took over control with the help of the able minister Bardas, and Theodora was shut up in a nunnery. This emperor has gone down in history as 'the Drunkard', but his reign was not without distinction, especially as an age of learning: the University of the Magnaura flourished and such men as the Patriarch Photius and the mathematician Leo brought renown to the capital. The most important event of Michael's reign, however, and the one that was to have the most lasting effect, was an attack on Constantinople from Russia in 860. It coincided with the first move towards the Christianisation of the southern Slavs by Cyril and Methodius and almost with the baptism of the Bulgar tsar in 864. From this time onwards the history of the Christian Slavs in the Balkans and of the Slavs of Russia, who were themselves to become Christians within just over a century, was to be closely linked with that of Byzantium. And with disputes with the Pope over the famous 'filioque' clause in the creed in 867 the future division of the Christian world into the Latin west and the Orthodox east was already virtually decided, even if the final split between the Churches did not come for almost another two centuries.

THE MACEDONIAN AGE

In the midst of these events, the final consequence of which was to exercise so great an influence on European history, the story of the Byzantine throne ran true to its somewhat gory form. Bardas was murdered in 865 by an upstart, Basil, who made himself co-emperor. In 867 he murdered Michael and came to the throne as sole emperor and founder of the great Macedonian dynasty. He was to reign till 886, his son Constantine being crowned as co-emperor in 869. In the west advances were at once made; Byzantine power was established to the east of the Adriatic and a new Dalmatian *theme* was founded; the position in Italy rapidly improved and terms were arrived at with the Papacy. In the east friendly relations were established with independent Armenia and some progress was made against the Arabs. But the gains made in the seventies were mostly lost again in the nineties, for the Byzantine forces suffered reverses in Italy, Sicily was finally lost, and in the east Armenia fell to the Arabs; in 904 the Arabs even sacked Salonica, though they made no attempt to hold it. The Bulgars took advantage of this situation to enlarge their territory, and for the next twenty years, under their ambitious and energetic tsar Simeon (d. 927), they proved a perpetual menace. In 907 a fleet from Russia once again appeared off Constantinople, and a new treaty was concluded.

Plate 59, *o* All this time the empire was ruled by Leo VI, the Wise (886–912), with Alexander as co-emperor. Economically it was an age of great prosperity, artistically it was outstanding. But it saw the beginnings of a gradual increase in the power of the aristocracy which was eventually to prove the ruin of the state, for by the end of the eleventh century the buying up of land by the great families had destroyed the system by which a sound peasantry and a territorial army were maintained as complements of one another, and the defence of the realm became a problem which was thereafter never really solved.

In spite of three marriages Leo had remained without a male heir and his efforts to marry a fourth time were violently resisted by the Church. He turned to the Pope for support, and was given absolution. But he died suddenly soon after, leaving Alexander as regent for the young emperor Constantine VII, Porphyrogenitus, the fruit of his fourth marriage. Alexander's inefficiency led to a palace revolution, and in 919 Romanus Lecapenus, the commander of the fleet, seized power, married his daughter to Constantine and had himself crowned as co-emperor. The more competent control of Romanus effectively checked Bulgarian advances, and with the death of the aggressive Bulgar tsar, Simeon, in 927 the whole situation was changed, for his successor Peter adopted a policy of peaceful co-existence. Romanus chose his subordinates well, and the empire was soundly governed. Though he was ready to take advantage of the aristocracy's prestige by marrying three of his sons into the great families – the fourth was made Patriarch – he nevertheless realised the danger of the threat to the smallholders and embarked on a bitter struggle against the growth of the great estates, passing severe laws to control land purchase by nobles and Church alike. But the power of the landowners had already grown so much that the laws were not wholly effective; indeed, the very people who were supposed to enforce the laws were often the very men who wished to secure land for themselves. Though his efforts in effecting these much-needed reforms were not wholly effectual, Romanus I's reign was a prosperous one. A threat by the Magyars in the west was foiled, a Russian landing in Bithynia in 941 was routed, and in the east quite considerable advances were made; in 944 the sacred Mandylion – the cloth bearing the imprint of Christ's face – which had been captured by infidels from Edessa, was rescued and brought to Constantinople; in a state where religion counted for so much this was an event of great importance.

But the same year was also marked by the arrest of the emperor by his sons and his exile to the Island of Prote, where he died as a monk in 948. The sons were arrested in turn, however, Constantine VII took control, and crowned his own son Romanus II as co-emperor in 945. The policy of Romanus I's government was maintained, though not always very successfully, and it cannot be claimed that Constantine was a great emperor from the political point of view. He was, however, an extremely interesting individual, a patron of the arts, a thinker and a prolific writer, and his *Book of Ceremonies* and *Book of the Prefect* are two of the most valuable source books that we have on life in the imperial palace and the organisation of the state at a time when Byzantine civilisation was at its apex.

Plate 38 In 959 Romanus II succeeded Constantine as sole emperor, and on his death in 963 Nicephorus Phocas, member of an aristocratic family and military commander, was proclaimed emperor by his troops; he at once legitimatised his position by marrying the elderly princess Theophano – another of those females on whom imperial descent depended, who run as a leit-motif through Byzantine history. In 969 she was to murder him and marry the more attractive John Tzimisces, who succeeded Nicephorus as emperor, though Theophano was banished by the Patriarch for her action. Nicephorus' rise to power meant a triumph for the aristocracy and the old laws to control them went by the board. Yet he did attempt to curb the growth of ecclesiastical estates which was having almost as serious results on the system of land ownership as the buying out of the peasant proprietors by the rich and powerful. He put a stop to any new monastic foundations, but permitted the development of old ones, and was himself the patron of the monastery of the Lavra on Mount Athos; a reliquary and gospel-cover which he presented survive there to this day. His policy was in some ways contradictory, for later he sought to increase the military holdings, realising their importance in the maintenance of defence. But if the civil administration had something of a dual character, and if the Emperor was in many ways callous and cruel, he was nevertheless a remarkably successful military commander, for Aleppo, Antioch and much of Syria were conquered and Cyprus was recaptured in 965. Affairs in the west presented dangers, however, for the Russian Sviatoslav, who had been persuaded to attack the Bulgars to effect the suitable balance of power that was always the keynote of Byzantine policy, had established himself in Bulgaria and become more of a danger than the Bulgars themselves. It remained for Nicephorus' successor, and murderer, John Tzimisces, to conquer Sviatoslav and annex Bulgaria before he died in 976. It was his kinswoman, another Theophano, who made history by becoming the wife of Otto II of Germany in 972.

The half-century that followed, covered by the reign of Basil II (976–1025), was one of the most prosperous in Byzantine history. It began by the crushing of a revolt in the east, when Basil was helped by Varangians from Russia; thereafter the Varangian guard was established as a vital part of the Byzantine army, though it was later recruited first from Scandinavia and then from Britain. The emperor was then free to turn his attention to the Balkans, and a series of campaigns, chiefly against the Bulgars, followed, though the main offensive was postponed till 1001 owing to a Fatimid attack on the eastern frontier in 995. The final defeat of the Bulgars was accomplished in 1014, Asia Minor was stabilised, territory in the Caucasus was annexed, the *themes* were reorganised, and the empire not only reached its greatest extent since the seventh century, but was also more stable at home and better governed. *Figs. 4, 5*

ZOE AND END OF THE MACEDONIAN DYNASTY

Nevertheless even Basil's strong hand was not able to check the growth of power of the aristocracy for long, and at his death the weak rule of the pleasure-loving Constantine VIII (1025–1028), who allowed the government to pass to others, and of his equally weak successor Romanus III (1028–1034), left the field open to a renewal of aristocratic influence. Constantine on his deathbed had married off Zoe, one of his three daughters, to Romanus to assure the succession, and again the empire came under the care of a characterful, if scheming and rather foolish, woman. Tiring of Romanus in 1034 she encouraged his murder by Michael of Paphlagonia, whom she at once married and had crowned as emperor. After a few years he retired to a monastery as a sick man and the throne was disputed till 1042, when Zoe came back with a third husband, Constantine IX Monomachos: after his death in 1055 Zoe's sister reigned for a year, but this was virtually the end of the great Macedonian dynasty. All these rulers had neglected the frontiers and dissi- Plate 82

Fig. 5. Themes *at the time of Basil II*

Th. CHERSON
PAPHLA-
GONIA
ARMENIAKON
CHALDIA
THEODOSIOPOLIS
IBERIA
COLONEA
SEBASTEIA
MESOPO-
TAMIA
TARON
VASPURAKAN
LARION
CHARSIANON
CAPPADOCIA
MELITENE
LYCANDUS
EUPHRATES
TELUCH
TOLIKON
CILICIA
TON
SELEUCIA
ANTIOCHEIA
CYPRUS
-HAS-

pated the finances, and their successors were confronted with a well-nigh insoluble problem – to reform the state and resist the mighty advances in east and west which the pendulum of fate had ordained at this time. But it was an intellectual age. A new university had been founded at Constantinople in 1045; Michael Psellos, perhaps the most distinguished writer that Byzantine civilisation produced, lived under Constantine Monomachos, and the emperor himself was a considerable patron of the arts. His superb enamel crown is to be seen at Budapest and his portrait in mosaic, along with that of his Empress, aged, but still youthful in appearance, survives in the south gallery of Haghia Sophia. It is especially interesting, for it was during this emperor's reign that the final and inevitable split between the Latin and Orthodox Churches came about in 1054.

Plate 76

THE FIRST COMNENES

The rising power of the aristocracy was illustrated by the crowning of Isaac Comnenus as the result of a *coup d'état* in 1057, for he was a member of one of the leading families. He took little interest in internal affairs, and the process of land acquisition by the nobles and the Church was allowed to continue unchecked. At the same time a new system, the *pronoia*, was introduced, which consisted in granting whole estates as a reward for military and other services. The taxes on these estates were collected by the holder, to be exploited by him to his own advantage. At first the grants were for life, but later the *pronoia* became hereditary and this brought further weakness, not to mention loss of revenue, to the state. And it was made even weaker militarily speaking by the fact that exemption from military service was permitted against a cash payment.

It is thus not surprising that the state was in no position to resist the threats that beset it on every hand, as new, progressive powers rose to prominence, the Normans in Sicily and southern Italy, the Petchenegs and Cumans in the north, and the Seljuk Turks in the east. The threat on the north, it is true, was perhaps no greater than that which had always existed since the days of

Justinian, as nomadic tribes pushed forward from the east, but the Normans and the Seljuks were both young, energetic and organised states, and both were thenceforth to play a very decisive part in history. Their rise coincided with the Byzantine decline, of which the history of the next twenty years was symptomatic.

In 1059 Isaac Comnenus' short reign was brought to an end mainly owing to the opposition of the Patriarch Cerularius – a sign of the growing power of the Church – and Constantine X Ducas, a member of another of the great aristocratic families, became emperor, with his wife Eudoxia, niece of Cerularius, as regent. On Constantine's death in 1068 she married the general Romanus Diogenes, who was crowned as Romanus IV. He was an emperor of considerable promise, and built a series of fortresses, each garrisoned by some 300 to 500 men, along the eastern frontier to resist the Seljuks. But after some initial successes he was defeated by them in the disastrous battle of Manzikert in 1071 and was captured. While he was a prisoner Eudoxia was deposed and sent to a nunnery by her eldest son, Michael, who was crowned emperor in 1071. Romanus, freed by the Seljuks, was captured and blinded by Michael and died the next year, being congratulated on achieving the happy state of martyrdom by Psellos, who had signed the order for his blinding.

After this somewhat dismal period, made equally depressing in the west by the loss of much of southern Italy to Robert Guiscard, came the longer and more prosperous reign of Alexius I Comnenus (1081–1118). The situation that confronted him was serious. In the west the Normans were advancing and were ready to attack the Balkans; in the north the Petchenegs had allied themselves with the Bulgars; in the east the Seljuks were already firmly established in Asia Minor. To remedy the situation Alexius sought allies in the west. The Venetians came to his aid, and Guiscard was defeated; but the

Plate 59, *p*

trading concessions granted to Venice as a reward were thereafter to prove a permanent millstone round Byzantium's neck. In the north Alexius got help from the Cumans, but they soon turned against him, though they were eventually dispersed. In the east on the other hand he succeeded in establishing friendly relationships with the Seljuks, who proved in the long run to be a less serious enemy than did the Latin Christians of the west.

THE FIRST AND SECOND CRUSADES

Confronted as the Byzantines were by the danger of war on three fronts, and distrustful as they had learnt to be of the Latin west, it is not at all surprising that the arrival in 1096 of the disorganised rabble of manhood, accompanied by a number of scheming and ambitious knights, which represented the First Crusade, was regarded with grave suspicion. That these westerners, brothers and cousins of Byzantium's bitter enemies in Italy, should have as their aim the capture of Syria and Palestine, which were regarded as legitimate parts of the Byzantine empire, only added to the suspicions with which the Byzantine emperor regarded them. Alexius' skill as a politician at once became apparent. He permitted the passage of the Crusaders towards the Holy Land, which removed them from the vicinity of his capital; he made them not only swear allegiance to him but also promise to hand over their gains, which gave him Nicaea in 1097; he followed in their wake with his own forces and captured several places from the Seljuks in Asia Minor when they were weakened by fighting against the Crusaders. But when the latter took Antioch in 1098 he was powerless, and it remained a part of the western crusading empire till it finally fell to Islam some two centuries later, an affront to the Byzantines and a source of the increasing mistrust with which they regarded the Latins.

Plate 59, n

Alexius was succeeded by John II (1118–1143), a prudent, clever and upright emperor of considerable literary ability, and for a time the situation remained stable. The Petchenegs were defeated in 1122 and Serbia recognised Byzantine overlordship. John conducted successful operations against Roger II in Sicily. He waged a gainful campaign against Cilician Armenia and he even thought of attacking Palestine, but was wounded by an arrow and died before he could do so. He was succeeded by his fourth son, Manuel II (1143–1180), a man of rather western tastes, married to a German princess who took the name of Irene. Manuel was soon unfaithful to her with his niece Theodora; his behaviour was in general somewhat frivolous, and it was his love of the west rather than any deep religious conviction that led to his efforts to bring about a union of the Churches. His policy was at first not unsuccessful; in the west, in spite of military advances by Roger II, Dalmatia and Croatia came under Byzantine control; in the east he procured the allegiance of Antioch. But the Second Crusade in 1147 was something of an embarrassment to him, and his reign was one of diplomatic bargaining which saw a constant re-alignment of powers, culminating in common action against the Byzantines on the part of Frederick Barbarossa and the Seljuks and the defeat of the Byzantine forces by the latter at Myriocephalum in 1176.

Manuel's efforts to improve the situation by diplomatic means had in fact really served to arouse suspicions on all sides; also intolerably high taxation caused discontent among the Byzantine population. It was probably as a result of both causes that there was a massacre of Latin settlers and sympathisers in Constantinople shortly after his death, though it was spurred on by Andronicus I as a means of obtaining the throne from the legitimate heir, Alexius II, the twelve-year-old son of the former friend of Manuel, who reigned with his western mother Theodora as regent. Andronicus was crowned as co-emperor, but a few months afterwards he strangled the unfortunate Alexius, and this brutal act was followed by a policy of severe and cruel oppression of the aristocracy. It was no doubt justified, but went too far; the great landowners resorted to arms and with the state racked by civil war the Latins attacked in the west, the Serbs and Hungarians conducted successful campaigns in the Balkans, and the Normans captured Salonica. Though Andronicus' oppression of the aristocracy had been combined with reforms in the system of tax collection aimed at relieving the lot of the people, he had also abolished circus games, and this had made him unpopular: in 1185, attributing the inevitable reverses to the emperor alone, the crowd attacked him and tore him to pieces.

Alexius I's daughter had married a member of the Angelus family, and their grandson Isaac II (1185–1195) now ascended the throne. It was said of him that he sold government posts like vegetables in a market. But perhaps he chose his buyers, for on the frontiers things improved slightly, the Normans were defeated in 1185, and in 1190 Stephen Nemanja of Serbia was beaten, though Serbia was tacitly recognised as an independent state. Isaac was again on the offensive in 1195, when he was deposed and blinded by his brother Alexius III (1195–1203), under whom affairs went from bad to worse. Indeed Alexius III's conduct, marked by ostentatious pomp at court and incompetence and dishonesty in government, really sealed the fate of the state. The Bulgarians defeated the Byzantine army in 1195 and Barbarossa's successor Henry VI was ready to launch an attack on a large scale when he died in 1197. Then, partly because of the Pope's call to a new Crusade, partly because of the promises made to Venice by Alexius, son of the deposed Isaac Angelus who hoped to gain the throne, but more as a result of the ambitions of Venice, a large expedition set out for Constantinople. After a brief delay to capture Zara on Venice's behalf, the Marmara was reached and Galata, already a Latin stronghold, was taken; the boom across the Golden Horn was broken, and when it appeared that the young Alexius was incapable of implementing his promises the western forces

THE FOURTH CRUSADE: CONSTANTINOPLE FALLS TO THE LATINS

attacked the city itself. On Good Friday 1204, the great centre of Christendom, which had resisted every threat of pagan and infidel since its foundation in 330, was sacked and looted by Christians who had ostensibly set out to free the Holy Cities of their faith. The protagonists in this action were the Venetians, and it was they too who reaped the principal gains, as the treasury of St Mark's attests to this day. The ascendency of Venice had begun some two hundred years before under Doge Orseolo II (991–1008); in 1204, under Dandolo, it reached its apogee and in the cultural sphere at least Venice became for a time the principal heir of Byzantium.

For a large portion of the population the rule of the Latins can have brought but little alteration. The *pronoias* were continued and for many of the holders brought nothing more than a change of allegiance, while for the ordinary people, once the immediate effects of looting in 1204 were forgotten, life must have continued much as before. But that was only for the unthinking. In the course of three days the vast treasure of art and literature that had been accumulated at Constantinople through the centuries was in greater part destroyed – what reached the west as loot represents a mere modicum of what perished. In those three days Christendom was finally split, never to be united however much pope or emperor might try to achieve unity. In those three days the Latins made for themselves implacable enemies at Constantinople and the Papacy became branded in Orthodox eyes with a stigma that survives to this day. Venice and her supporters may have gained a brief victory and much booty – but they also sealed the fate of east Christian Europe and opened the way for the Turkish conquests of the fifteenth century and to a large extent determined the isolation of Russia till the time of Peter the Great.

If some of the *pronoia* holders and the landowners or merchants were ready to accept the new overlordship, the majority of the upper classes were antagonistic, and when Theodore Lascaris set up his court at Nicaea many resorted thither to his support, the Patriarch amongst them. At the same time a revolt against the Latins began in Thrace, and a separate Orthodox emperor, a member of the old Comnene family, was enthroned at far-distant Trebizond, with the support of the Georgian queen Tamara. Though the empire at Trebizond was to last till 1461, that of Theodore Lascaris at Nicaea was really the more important, and soon began to flourish. He succeeded in resisting attacks by the Seljuks and in 1214 made treaties which resulted in a balance of power between them and the Latins.

More serious opposition was to confront him from another refuge of Orthodoxy that had been established in Greece, namely the independent despotate of Epirus, which had been founded by Michael Angelus. In 1215 he was succeeded by the ambitious and energetic Theodore Angelus Ducas Comnenus – to give him his full name – who claimed relationship with all the great imperial families of the past. He captured Salonica from the Latins in 1224 and thereupon claimed all the rights and titles of the Byzantine Emperor. Theodore Lascaris of Nicaea had at about the same time been succeeded by John III Vatatzes (1222–1254), a man of great energy who not only drove the Latins out of Asia but also invaded Thrace and captured Adrianople. Realising the danger that Vatatzes presented to the future of the more westerly kingdom, Theodore Angelus attacked him in the rear and forced him to withdraw. At this point Theodore Angelus almost had Constantinople within his grasp, but he in turn was attacked by the Bulgarian tsar John Asen II (1218–1241), and was captured and blinded. Nothing could have suited Vatatzes better, for his principal rival had been eliminated at no cost to himself. He consequently made a treaty with John Asen, and himself launched an attack on Constantinople in 1236, but Asen changed sides and Vatatzes withdrew before the city could be captured. In 1241 Asen died, and the way seemed open for Vatatzes, but he was forced to turn his attentions to the east by the Mongol advance into Asia Minor. In 1246, however, the Mongols withdrew, and Vatatzes was once more free to concern himself with the west; he captured Salonica and parts of the Bulgarian empire, but he died before he was able to tackle the main problem of Constantinople. He had, nevertheless, set his empire on a sound military and financial footing, agriculture was prosperous, the poor were well and justly treated, and he had organised an efficient system of defensive castles along his eastern frontier.

His successor Theodore II Lascaris (1254–1258) was to make Nicaea a centre of culture and literature in addition, and even if he did little in the military way his reign marked the summit of the Nicaean achievement. But the emperors, and their subjects too, were not content with Nicaea. Constantinople was the real goal, and progress in the political sphere came when Michael VIII Palaeologus was crowned as co-emperor with Theodore's true heir, John IV, in 1259. Two years later Constantinople was retaken, Michael was crowned for a second time in Haghia Sophia, and his son, Andronicus, aged three, was proclaimed Basileus and legitimate heir. This marked the access to power of a new dynasty, the Palaeologan, the longest lived of any Byzantine line, for it outlasted the Macedonian by five years. Plate 59, *r*

The years between about 1250 and 1300 had seen some of the most complicated political manoeuvrings of the whole of Byzantine history. Michael Palaeologus was an adept at intrigue, and his very great abilities were called on to the full, not only to cope with complications and rival demands in the Greek world, but also to deal with Venetian, Genoese, Angevin and Papal claims and counterclaims on his territory. The Angevins, first as rulers of Sicily and then in the Peloponnese, were probably his most dangerous opponents; with the popes he succeeded in remaining in the main on good terms, and between 1274 and 1278 was actively concerned in plans to bring about the unification of the Orthodox and Roman

Churches. Though he was no doubt more interested in the political repercussions of these approaches, he was, it would seem, also sincerely desirous of healing the breach, but intransigence on the part of the popes and deep-rooted opposition in the Greek world prevented any lasting arrangement.

UNREST AND WARS

But though a master of diplomacy, Michael was not able to avoid active hostilities and the last half of the thirteenth century was marked by incessant campaigns, more especially in Greece, the Morea and the Islands; only in the east, where the Seljuk Turks ruled as vassals of the Mongols, was there comparative tranquillity. The Latin Christians, not the Moslems, were really the Orthodox Christians' most bitter foes. To follow out the endless ding-dong of these campaigns is a thankless task; their cost must have been considerable and the drain that they exercised on state resources must have been far in excess of any material, even political, gains for which they were responsible. What is amazing, as one reads the pages of history, is that life can have continued at all in any normal manner during these fifty years. Yet a surprising number of churches and other buildings were set up and decorated at that time and these are in many ways some of the most important years in Byzantine cultural and artistic history.

It was in the east that Michael's political prowess had its most advantageous effects. The keynote there was provided by the Mongols, for in the very same year that he was crowned Hulagu had taken Baghdad, which at once put pressure on the Turks from behind. Michael concluded an alliance with the Mongols of the Golden Horde in Russia in 1271 as well as with the Mamluks of Egypt, both of them opposed to Hulagu, so creating a balance of power which stabilised affairs for a time. Western aggression was also halted by a pact with the pope in 1274, but the ascendency of the Angevins continued and things would have been very serious for Michael had not the course of events been interrupted by a chance occurrence, the Sicilian vespers, which put an end to French ascendency in that island and consequently to western aspirations in the Balkans. Michael, however, was not strong enough to return to the offensive; he died soon after, and his son Andronicus II (1282–1328) came to the throne. Plate 59, g

His task was no easy one. The west was itching to attack Byzantium and the Constantinople of the first Palaeologues must have appeared from the western angle much like the Istanbul of the later nineteenth century, 'the sick man of Europe'. The cost of maintaining the large mercenary army which was necessary to hold the eastern frontier was beyond the powers of the state; the economic position was extremely serious; taxation was heavy and the people and the small landowners were in a bad way. As a result the coinage was debased, but this did not really stop the rot, for the owners of the great estates thought only of themselves and the *pronoia* holders became if anything better off in that their grants were made hereditary. Added to these difficulties there were constant internal squabbles for power, which culminated in the crowning of Andronicus III as co-emperor in 1325; he became sole emperor three years later. He was gallant and energetic, but two new enemies appeared on the scene, Serbia under the ambitious and able Dushan, and the Ottoman Turks, who defeated the Byzantines in 1331 and thereafter soon dominated the whole of northern Asia Minor. The Byzantines came to an understanding with the Seljuks and achieved some success, and they also gained ground in Greece, especially against the Genoese, who, after helping the Palaeologues to power, had sought to gain more and more in the way of territory and concessions. But civil war broke out on the death of Andronicus III in 1341, for his son and heir John V was only nine years old, and the ground that had been gained during his reign was rapidly lost.

The struggle was perhaps inevitable, for it was directed to some extent against the excessive power of the aristocratic

Plate 94

Plate 95

families, but it was brought to a head by the rivalries of two great men, John Cantacuzenus, who had controlled civil affairs during the reign of Andronicus II, and the Lord High Admiral Apocaucos. Cantacuzenus, helped first by the Serbians, and then by the Turks, ousted Apocaucos and was crowned at Adrianople in 1346; the next year he entered Constantinople to be crowned again there as John VI. His reign was short as well as difficult. In 1348 a severe plague broke out which further reduced not only the population but also the wealth of the state, and throughout trouble continued with the faction of the Hesychasts, a group of religious mystics, which had played a part in the civil wars that brought Cantacuzenus to the throne. The emperor was not popular, and in 1354 he was forced to abdicate and retired to a monastery. It is characteristic of the age that both his and Apocaucos' memory is recorded for us through their artistic patronage, as was that of another official, Theodore Metochites, builder of the lovely Kariye Camii a generation before, whereas practically nothing remains to recall the munificence or taste of the emperors of the direct line.

ATTEMPTS TO REUNITE THE CHURCHES

With Cantacuzenus' death the reign of John V, which had been interrupted by the former's revolt, recommenced; it was to be interrupted again by his son Andronicus IV between 1376 and 1379 and by John VII in 1390. Andronicus captured Constantinople with the support of the Genoese, and John V was forced to turn to the Turks to regain his throne. John's main aim throughout his troubled reign, during much of which he was virtually a vassal of the Turks, was the union of the Churches. He made a journey to Italy to further this cause and was himself converted to Rome in 1369, but the Church at home – by now more influential than the emperor – would not ratify his actions. Nor were his promises taken very seriously in the west and, height of ignominy, he, the emperor of Byzantium, was arrested as a common debtor at Venice on the way home. But it was the vassalage to the Turks which brought about the severest loss of face, and it was because of this, as much as because of the impoverished state of the empire, that Manuel II (1391–1425), John V's successor, was again unable to obtain any help when he made his famous journey to Italy, France and England in search of support in 1399. He was, however, universally respected as a man and it is an irony of fate that this brave, able, cultured personality, the only one of John V's sons who had remained true to his father, was left without support, and when the Turks were defeated by the Mongols in 1402 the Byzantines were too weak to profit from the occasion, and the best they could obtain was a treaty of non-aggression signed by Suleiman in 1403, which was respected by the Turks for nearly twenty years.

Granted this respite, Manuel was able to turn to home affairs and in 1415 he visited Mistra in the Peloponnese, the most flourishing part of his realm. This little city had succeeded not only in retaining its independence in the midst of a number of Latin principalities, but had also become the most vital centre of culture in the Near East, where art and letters flourished to a degree unequalled in Constantinople since the great period in the tenth and eleventh centuries. But its days, like those of the capital, were numbered, and though it remained independent till 1463 it was constantly threatened and in danger.

TURKISH OFFENSIVES: THE END OF CONSTANTINOPLE

In 1421 the Turks turned again to the offensive and much of the Peloponnese was sacked. But once more they were deflected from Mistra and Constantinople by troubles in Asia Minor; once more the emperor sought help in the west and proposed a union of the Churches, for Manuel's successor John VIII (1425–1448) went to Italy in 1437; once again what the emperor proposed was not to be conceded by the Church and the only result was a further loss of face in the Orthodox world; once more a brief respite was given, thanks to the ambitions of Hunyadi in Hungary and Scanderbeg in Albania, who both violently resisted Turkish incursions which had now enveloped the western Balkans. But the respite was brief. John VIII died in 1438 and his successor was crowned at Mistra as Constantine XI. Three years later Mohammed II succeeded Murad as Sultan of the Turks, and his first avowed aim was to put an end to a situation which had become quite illogical. Again Constantine sought help in the west; again the Orthodox Church refused to consider union. 'Better the turban of the Moslem in the midst of Constantinople than the mitre of the Latin,' stated a high official. And so it was to be. In 1453, after one of the most gallant defences of history, the city fell and the last of the Constantines died gloriously in the midst of the fighting to defend the city founded by the first of the name one thousand one hundred and twenty-three years before.

So ended the glorious, fascinating and at times almost repulsive tale of the Byzantine emperors. No historical record shows so surprising a mingling of gallantry and treachery, competence and inefficiency, piety and opportunism. In no other sphere of the tale of Byzantine civilisation is the strange duality that stood as the very essence of Byzantine culture more marked. It is the story of an empire that at one time embraced the whole of the civilised world of the west within its realm; which was the chief centre of the world's thought and culture for some nine hundred years, and which existed in its own right as an empire for more than a thousand. It is the story of a state in which the Church was as powerful as the emperor, at a time when emperors were all-powerful, and which was more influenced as regards its daily life by the Christian faith than any other state in the Christian era. Yet it is at the same time the story of an imperial succession, where the emperors came to the throne only too often by murdering their rivals, and where they frequently maintained their position by treachery, intrigue and cruelty. It is the story of a nation which does not fall into one of the simple categories of the Marxist ideology, where a state of serfdom is supposed to give way to one of feudalism, one of feudalism to one of capitalism and so on. The Byzantine state was never one of serfdom, though there were slaves; though the families of the powerful gained a great deal of influence from the eleventh century onwards, it was never truly feudal. It was certainly never either bourgeois or capitalist. It was imperial and it was Christian, and the two were made to combine to produce a way of life that was never exactly paralleled elsewhere. The history of no other state shows quite the same union of opposites, that of no other culture quite the same blend of the material and the spiritual. Dualism is the keynote, and to describe justly the Byzantine world Engels would have to add this new category to his list of societies.

CHAPTER IV

Their Architecture

Thanks be to God who has found me worthy to complete so great a work and to surpass even thee, O Solomon.

JUSTINIAN, on the completion of Haghia Sophia

ORIGINS OF THE BYZANTINE STYLE

BYZANTINE ARCHITECTURE is perhaps the most clearly defined and distinctive style in Europe. It owed, certainly, a considerable debt to pagan Rome, more especially to the great vaulted buildings of brick which were favoured by many of the emperors for their baths, palaces and public edifices. It owed a debt to early Christian art as developed by Constantine and his immediate successors in the great three-aisled basilicas like Sta Sabina or Sta Maria Maggiore at Rome. It owed a debt to hither Asia, where experiments in the elaboration of the square plan as a building entity had been in progress since the third century, especially in Syria. It also owed a debt to Iran, where an individual system of vault construction and an elaborate domical architecture had been developed under the patronage of the Sasanian emperors (222–650). But as early as the time of Justinian these diverse elements had been blended to compose a style which was no mere eclectic mixture, but rather a profound and complete fusion of available elements, accomplished at the behest of the Christian Church and brought about thanks to the patronage of the Byzantine emperor, Christ's vice-regent on earth.

It was perhaps to some extent the result of chance that all the factors necessary to effect the fusion of these elements were brought into play at a given moment shortly before the middle of the sixth century. Christian thought had by then been formulated along specific lines, and though there were still to be many arguments as to the exact nature of belief, dissident heretical sects breaking off, especially in the east, the main tenets of Orthodoxy had been established and the type of church-plan and the nature of the interior that was considered most desirable to meet the Churches' needs was coming to be realised. The architect, as much as the artist, had been taken under the wing of the Church, and even if no direct architectural specifications had been propounded, it was coming to be realised that the needs of eastern Orthodoxy were very particular, and that what had been acceptable to Rome was not necessarily suitable for the new capital at Constantinople or for the great cities of the eastern empire which were to a great extent dependent on the capital. In early Christian times the longitudinal hall, in which the gaze of the worshipper was automatically directed towards the altar at the end – at first not necessarily at the eastern end – of the building had seemed satisfactory. But in the Byzantine sphere, where a new, more transcendental outlook dominated the thought-world, something distinct and more imaginative was called for, and it must have seemed that the need could only be supplied by a type of building that would also direct the gaze upwards and the thoughts heavenward. Experiments had already been made with roofing forms that would satisfy these demands both in Rome and in the east, namely the dome and the vault. These were possessed of an imaginative, poetic appeal quite absent in the simple timbered roof used on the basilicas. The distinction of Byzantine architecture was that it perfected the use of these two forms in association, producing thereby an imaginative, wholly organic style.

A great deal has been written on the question of the origin of the dome and where it was first employed on a large scale, one school of thought assigning the credit for its origin to the eastern Mediterranean and another to Italy. Certainly the earliest large example that survives is the Pantheon at Rome, but

the foundations of similar structures which are to be dated to Hellenistic or early Roman times have been found at Pergamon and Constantinople, though their roofs and upper walls have
Fig. 6 perished; it is quite possible that these examples from the east Mediterranean sphere antedate those in the Roman. But these are all domes over a circle, and they stand to some extent outside the line of development which was essential if the dome was to be used in association with a plan which would permit of greater development than the circle. The problem, in fact,

Fig. 6. Circular building near the Myrelaion, Constantinople. Plan. Probably first century

was to find some way of setting the circular dome above a building of square or rectangular plan, for the square could be elaborated in numerous ways by extending one or more of its sides, to produce such variants as an apsed square, an apsed rectangle, a cruciform building, or an open square composed of columns within a second closed square.

The problem had already been solved either on a small scale or in a rather primitive way well before Justinian's day, and two distinct methods were in existence, both of which were to
Fig. 7 survive for many centuries. One is known as the squinch, the other as the pendentive and, curiously enough, early examples of each are to be found in the same building, the church at Abu Mina near Alexandria. The first, the squinch, consisted

in building what was virtually an arch across the open corner formed by topping a square base with arches on each of its four sides. The square was in this way turned into an octagon, and this in turn approached nearly enough to a circle to permit of the base of the dome, or its drum, being erected upon it. It was, however, not wholly satisfactory, for the ends of the squinch rested on the middles of the main spanning arches, so exercising a thrust at what was obviously a point of weakness.

Fig. 7. The squinch. After C. Stewart

The other method, the pendentive, was more satisfactory, for it served to bind the spanning arches together rather than to force them apart. It was formed by placing in each of the four spaces between the main arches that topped the square a triangle of masonry with curved sides, two of them corresponding to the curves of the arches supporting the dome, the third forming the base of one quadrant of the circle on which it rested. *Fig. 8*

The two methods were more or less equally common and examples of both are to be found in east and west alike, but it is perhaps safe to regard the pendentive as an Hellenistic invention and the squinch as an eastern development, for it was used on quite a large scale in Sasanian Persia, for example in the palace of Firuzabad, which was erected as early as AD 224.

Similarly, two methods of vaulting had been developed well before Constantine's time. One, the Roman, was the more efficient, but it could only be built with the aid of an elaborate wooden centring, the bricks or stones of which it was made

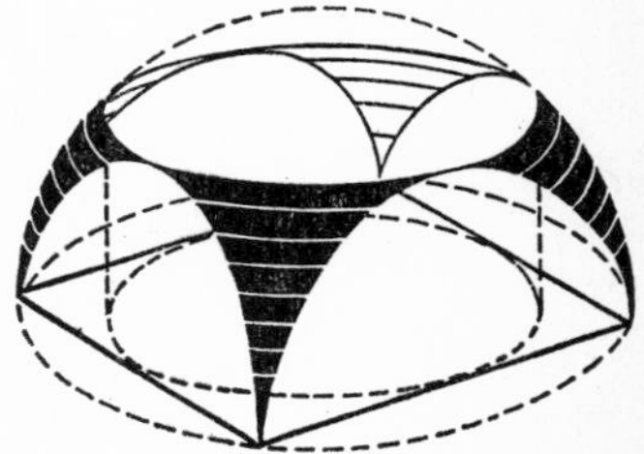

Fig. 8. The pendentive. After C. Stewart

being set parallel with the side walls, in a bedding of hard
cement. In the other, the eastern, the bricks were set at right
angles to the side walls, and as they were inclined at an angle,
it was possible to build the vault out from a back wall, laying
one brick upon the other, without centring. The method is
usually described as that of 'pitching'. We find the two systems
used together in the same roof in some of the substructures of
Plate 10 the Great Palace of the Emperors at Constantinople which are
probably to be dated to the time of Justinian. The example is
important, for it serves to show that the masons of the capital
were familiar with both eastern and Roman methods. Other
substructures in the palace and elsewhere show that they were
also familiar with another Roman method, that of using con-
Plate 12 crete in mass within a wooden or other casing, in much the
same way as reinforced concrete is set today, though rough
stones, bricks or building debris were also used in the mixture.

BUILDING METHODS

Another building method often employed in earlier times,
though not so much after the seventh century, was the use of
Plate 17 large stone blocks. It was probably this that suggested to the
Byzantine masons a method which became especially characteristic of their work in Constantinople; here a given number
Plate 11 of courses of brick alternate with one or more of stone. When
the work was intended to be seen the pointing was also very
carefully done, so that the masonry itself was a thing of real
beauty. This is the case in the land walls of the city, set up
Plate 1 under Theodosius II between 413 and 477. There are considerable variations in the number of brick and stone courses and
in the ways in which the pointing is finished off, and it is
sometimes possible for the expert to hazard a date for a building
on the basis of the technique of its construction. As yet, however, the evidence has not been fully collated. More reliable as
a dating factor are the stamps with which the bricks are often
marked, but even here there is a good deal of uncertainty as to
Fig. 9 how they should be interpreted.

Fig. 9. Brick stamp from Constantinople. Walker Trust excavations

JUSTINIAN'S PATRONAGE AND CHURCHES

Building methods were thus advanced and varied by Justinian's time, and experiments in which domes and vaults had both been used on quite a large scale had already been made. In the west, San Lorenzo at Milan, an apsed square on columns within a closed apsed square, had already been roofed with a large dome in the third quarter of the fifth century. In the east there had been a great deal of church building, and experiments in projecting the sides of the square to produce the embryo of a cruciform plan had already taken place. But the empire had lacked cohesion and the emperors driving spirit until a man who was at once capable of restoring the empire and inspiring a whole series of new enterprises in church building appeared on the scene in the person of Justinian. And in the capital a sudden need to rebuild came about as a result of the destruction of a large part of the city, including its great cathedral of the Holy Wisdom, in the course of the Nika riots of 532.

Fig. 10

Seldom in the whole history of architecture had an opportunity for the development of a wholly new style been so

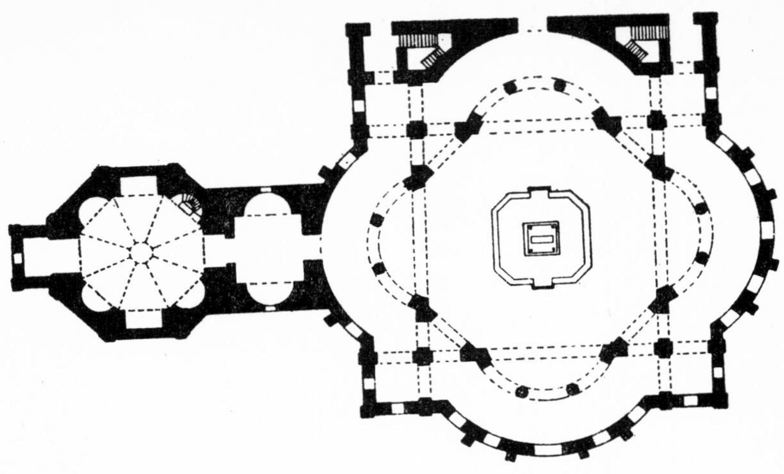

Fig. 10. St Lorenzo, Milan. Plan. Fourth century. After Rubach

temptingly presented. Never before or probably never since was such an opportunity so ably exploited. Within a few years a whole series of buildings of world-wide significance in the story of architectural development had been erected, each of them solving in a different way the problem of combining in one structure the ground plan of a three-aisled basilica, which had been sanctioned for the Christian Church by custom, and the domed or vaulted roof, which made possible a completely new conception of interior space and permitted a visionary approach truly in keeping with the tenets of the new faith as it had been developed at Constantinople. A whole series of changes on the combination of these two ideas were rung by Justinian's architects, not only in the capital but in the most far-flung sections of the empire also, in such places as Ephesus or the Greek Islands, Ravenna or the Holy cities of Palestine.

Justinian was responsible for building four major churches in Constantinople; three of them survive to this day. There were certainly others which have disappeared leaving little or no trace. Each of those that we know shows, in its own way, a fresh and distinct solution of the building problems which confronted the architects of Christendom at the time. The first was still to some extent experimental, namely the church of SS. Sergius and Bacchus, set up between 526 and 537. Basically it is an open-sided octagon of two stories, topped by a dome, and enclosed within a square, from one side of which projects a small presbytery, while on the other there is a transverse narthex. San Vitale at Ravenna, also built under Justinian's patronage, is akin, but the presbytery is larger and the inner octagon is enclosed in an octagon instead of a square. The plan of both churches is effective, but is also to some extent conservative, in that it represents a variation, though an advanced one, on that of the old type of martyrium like Sta Constanza at Rome (324–326), and does not really permit either of great extension in size or of any change from a wholly centralised disposition. It is the sculptures of the interior of SS. Sergius and Bacchus, the delicate cornices and the lovely capitals, that show most clearly the strides that the new art was making, for their whole essence is fresh and original, and contrasts as markedly with sculptures of the Roman phase as do the paintings of a Raphael with a Romanesque doorway.

Fig. 11
Plate 13

The church of St Eirene (532) shows greater ingenuity, for here the three-aisled plan of the early basilicas has been retained on the ground, but above there is a great dome over the main square, with today a second dome roofing an area to the west of it, only slightly smaller than the main one. Both are set on massive brick piers which take the place of some of the columns of the normal three-aisled basilica. Indeed, the idea of alternating a built pier with every three or four columns had already been tried out in basilicas with timber roofs in the east, as for instance in St Demetrius at Salonica, presumably to give greater stability in an area where earthquakes were not unusual. Thus the architect of St Eirene successfully combined a plan that best served the demands of the Christian faith, in that it

Fig. 12
Plate 16

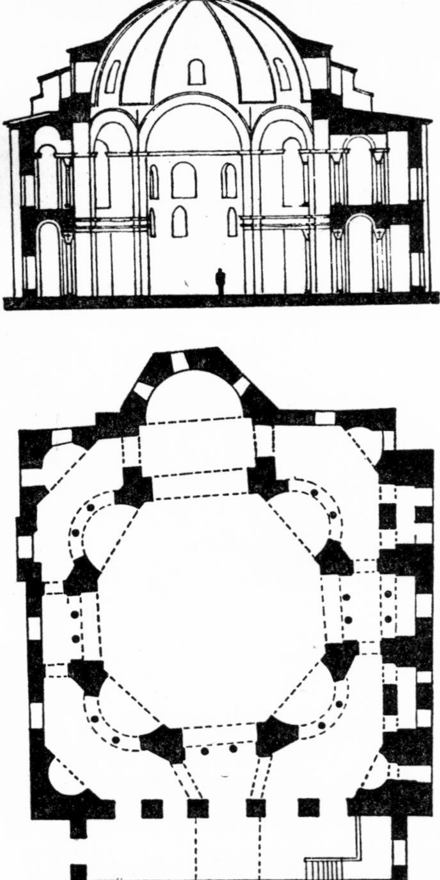

Fig. 11. SS. Sergius and Bacchus, Constantinople. Plan. 526–537. After Van Millingen

provided plenty of space for the congregation and a worthy setting for the liturgy, with a form of roof which gave the building great glory, suggesting to the worshipper the idea of the vault of heaven, which the esoteric thought of Byzantium demanded. The same theme was further developed in the church of the Hundred Doors on the Island of Paros, which is also to be assigned to Justinian's day. But the area below the dome was here extended, so that the ground plan seems to resemble that of two three-aisled basilicas intersecting at right angles, with a dome at the point of intersection. The result is somewhat clumsy, but it contains a great new idea in embryo: the large-scale cruciform building. This was further developed in the church of the Holy Apostles at Constantinople.

Here the association between religious conceptions and architecture was carried even further. The three-aisled ground plan was retained on the west–east axis, but the area was roofed by three domes, that at the centre being rather larger than the other

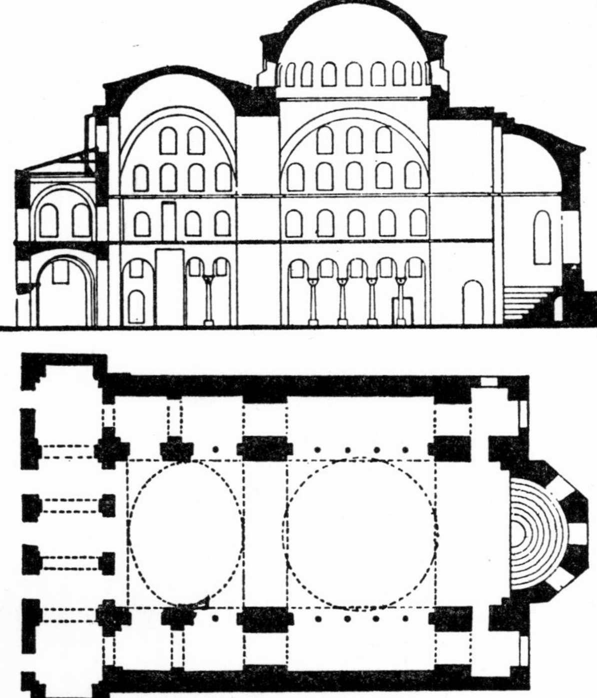

Fig. 12. St Eirene, Constantinople. Plan. 532. After Van Millingen

two, while the idea that the placing of a dome on four columns must have automatically suggested was carried to a logical conclusion by building out a transept on either side. Thus a truly cruciform plan resulted, and as the transepts were also domed a new type, the five-domed church, came into being. Justinian's church of the Holy Apostles was the prototype. It has, alas, perished, but its plan was repeated in St Mark's at Venice, and that church probably served in turn as the model for others in the west, like St Front at Périgueux. A variant on the prototype is to be seen in the church of St John at Ephesus, where there is one dome at the crossing, one each on the northern, eastern and southern arms, and two on the much longer western extension. On plan the building thus heralds the abbeys and cathedrals of the Romanesque age in the west, though the domes are distinctive.

Fig. 13 *Fig. 14*

HAGHIA SOPHIA

It was, however, reserved for Justinian's architect Anthemius of Tralles to produce the most ambitious and original solution

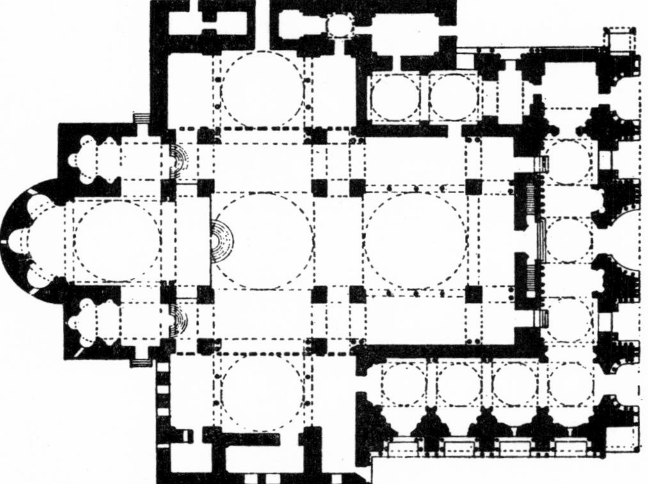

Fig. 13. St Mark's, Venice. Plan. Eleventh century. After Rubach

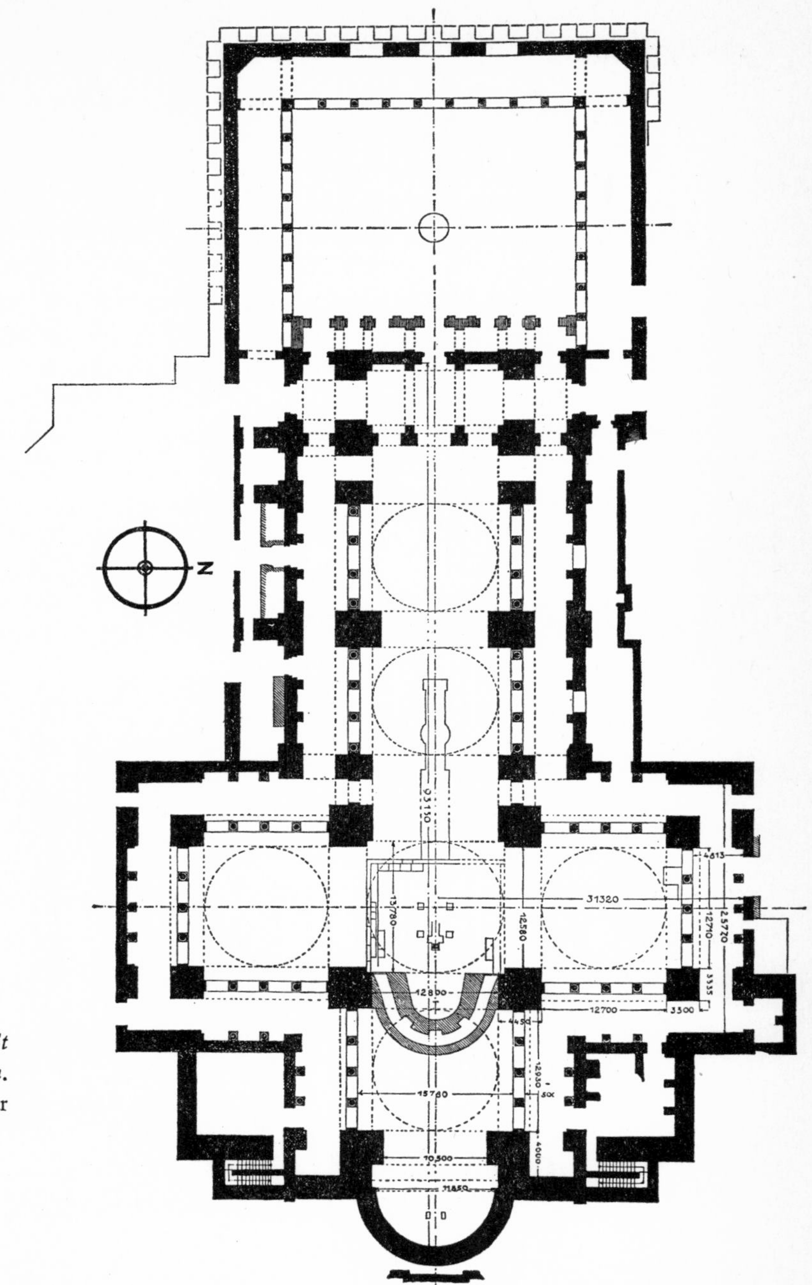

Fig. 14. Church of St John, Ephesus. Plan. Sixth century. After Wiegand

to the problem of combining the three-aisled ground plan with a roof of wholly imaginative quality, for in the great cathedral
Plate 18 of the Holy Wisdom, Haghia Sophia, he conceived the idea of
Fig. 15 enlarging the size of the central area and putting a great semi-dome at either end of it, so giving an impression of length and at the same time building a dome which has for ever remained the wonder of all. It seemed to be suspended on invisible chains from heaven, said one early writer, and its effect was at once appreciated as something not only glorious but also to some
Plate 19 extent miraculous. It was described in glowing terms by a court official, John the Silentiary, and his words are worthy of quotation:

> Whoever raises his eyes to the beauteous firmament of the roof, scarce dares to gaze on its rounded expanse, sprinkled with the stars of heaven, but turns to the fresh green marble below . . . Whoever puts foot within the sacred fane would live there forever, and his eyes well with tears of joy. Thus by divine counsel, while angels watched, was the temple built again.

Procopius, the historian, similarly attributed the credit to the Almighty:

> Whoever enters there to worship [he wrote] perceives at once that it is not by any human strength or skill, but by the favour of God, that this work has been perfected.

And he goes on to describe its earthly beauties as well as its
Plates 14, 15 heavenly glory. Its sculptured capitals and cornices are in a new and distinctive style; its plan was wholly original, for one of the truly great strides in architectural development had been taken. The manner of the sculptures was followed in much subsequent Byzantine work, but the building itself seemed so perfect, so complete, that no efforts were thereafter made, by Byzantine architects at least, to emulate it.

From Justinian's day onwards the dome remained the essential factor of Byzantine church building, though its form varied.

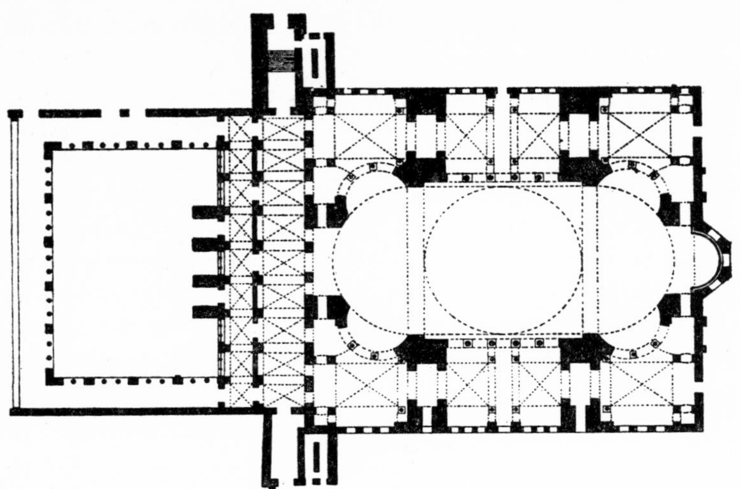

Fig. 15. Haghia Sophia, Constantinople. Plan. 532–537. After Salzenberg

CHURCHES OF THE MACEDONIAN AGE

But planners sought new variations on the theme and in the great age of the Macedonian emperors (ninth/eleventh centuries) usually tended towards greater complication. Even so during the three centuries that separated this period from the age of Justinian little progress was made and little in the way of innovation was attempted. At first the lack of enterprise was probably to be attributed to economic causes, for Justinian left the treasury empty and his successors were hard put to it to make both ends meet, especially in view of the needs of defence, for through much of the next two centuries the empire was assailed on all sides. Then, in 717, the first of the Iconoclast emperors came to the throne, and though the disputes that racked the state had reference to art rather than to architecture, it would seem that little in the way of church building was done; when it was, nothing was attempted on a large scale, and simple materials and sober ornament replaced the rich marbles and lavish decorations of Justinian's day. Thus piers built of brick were in

the seventh and eighth centuries more usual than marble columns, and sculpture was avoided. But with the end of Iconoclasm in 843 building began once more, and though much that was done in this period has now perished, a few of the larger and more impressive churches still stand. The mon-
Plate 23 astery churches of Hosios Lukas, near Delphi in Greece and
Plate 20 that of Daphni near Athens may be cited. Many churches once existed in Constantinople, but none survives there in its pristine state.

It was however not so much by grandeur of conception or thanks to the imaginative solution of constructional problems that these later churches were distinguished, but rather by an elaboration of plan and an ornateness of detail. The builders also seem to have liked adding to the buildings of earlier times;
Fig. 16 the church of Christ Pantocrator at Constantinople is thus
Fig. 17 really three churches side by side, that of St Mary Panachrantos is a double church, with side gallery and outer narthex of later date, and there are two intercommunicating churches in the
Fig. 18 monastery of Hosios Lukas, one of slightly earlier date than the other. Numerous other examples of this tendency could be cited, though Byzantine churches never assumed the same complexity of plan as those in Georgia, where the architects became obsessed with the problem of devising complicated geometric figures on the ground, almost regardless of the effect that the buildings would produce in elevation.

This business of enlarging existing buildings by duplication seems to have preoccupied builders especially during Macedonian and Comnene times, though many of the churches of the age were small, telling primarily because of their balanced proportions; that at Nerez in Yugoslavia, dating from about
Plate 21 1164, is typical. With the restoration of the empire under the Palaeologues in 1261 a new style of architecture came into vogue characterised by small, rather intimate interiors, by the presence of narrow domes on tall drums, and by a love of ornate

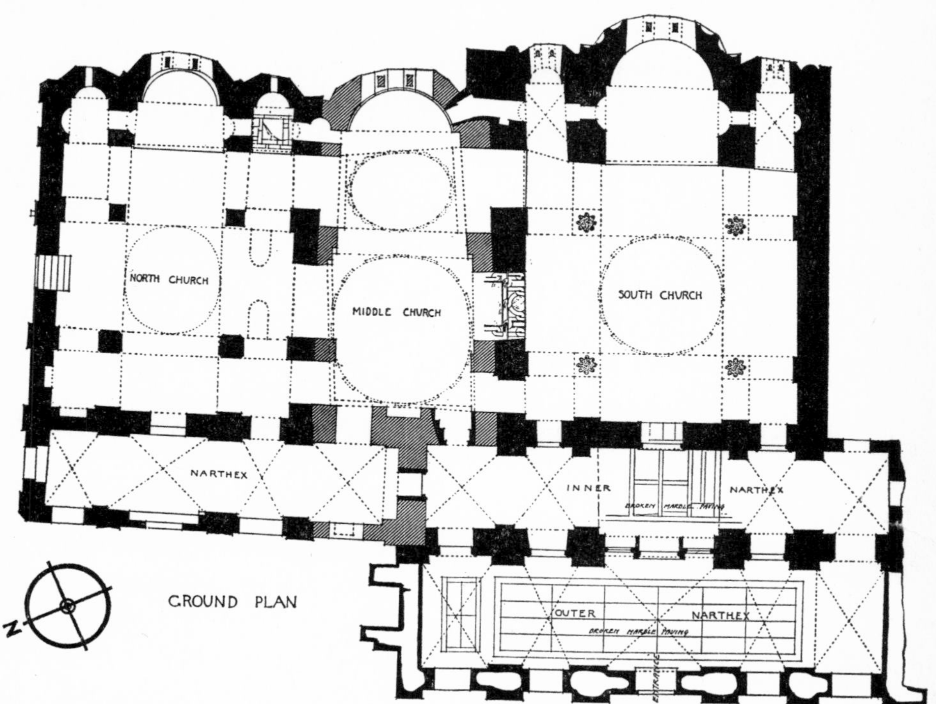

Fig. 16. Church of Christ Pantocrator, Constantinople. Plan. After Van Millingen

exteriors. As time went on the buildings also tended to become higher in comparison to their size on plan. The early fourteenth century was especially active, and there survive quite a number of churches which were set up around the year 1310. In Greece, as in the church of the Holy Apostles at Salonica (1312–1315), ornamental brickwork was highly favoured as a form of external decoration. In Constantinople elaborate arcading was more usual, as at the east end of Kariye Camii. Another characteristic of the age was the use of domes as a roofing for side chapels and subsidiary structures, as in the Holy Apostles at Salonica. This

Plate 24
Fig. 19
Plate 22

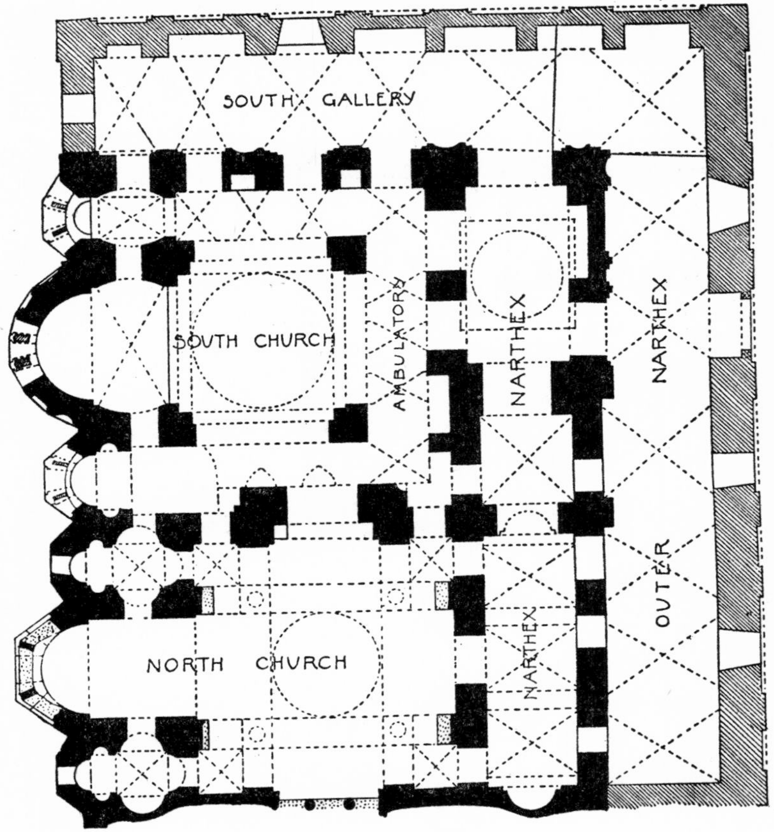

Fig. 17. Church of St Mary Panachrantos, Constantinople. Plan. After Van Millingen

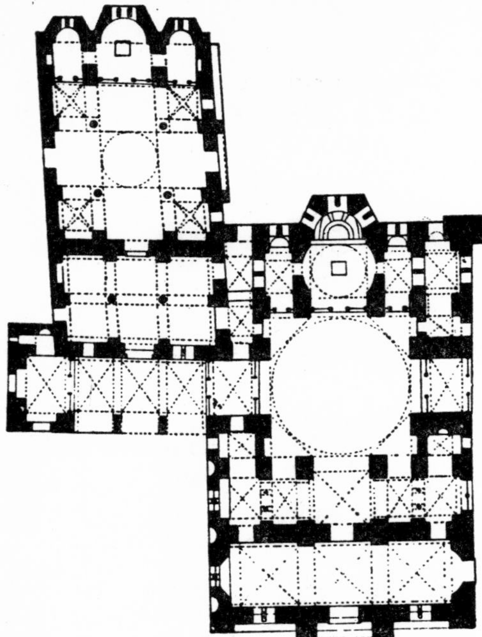

Fig. 18. The two churches of the monastery of Hosios Lukas, in Phocis, Greece. Plan. Eleventh century. After Schultz

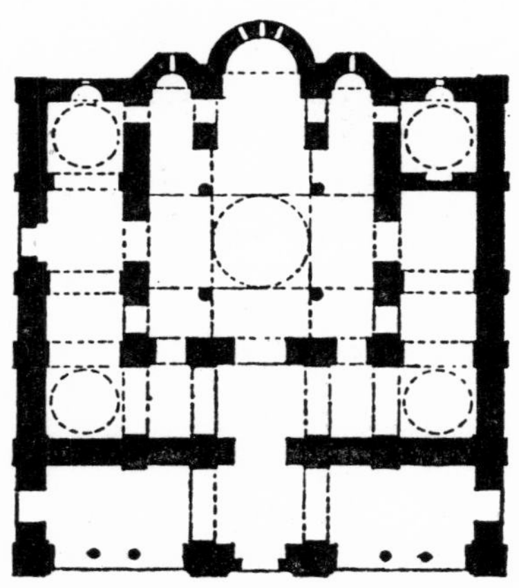

Fig. 19. Church of the Holy Apostles, Salonica. Plan. c. *1312*

fourteenth-century style is a very distinctive one. Like late Gothic it may be described as feminine rather than very masculine, telling by charm and delight rather than through monumentality or magnificence. But like late Gothic it is very delightful and well worthy of close consideration.

THE PALAEOLOGUE AGE

It is perhaps not surprising that a great deal of building was done in the young states of Bulgaria and Serbia, where the rulers sought to assert their independence by acts of patronage, but it is a striking tribute to the recuperative powers of Byzantine civilisation that so many fine churches should have been set up in Constantinople, in Salonica and in Greece in the last phase of the empire's history, when its wealth was sorely diminished. Churches of the fourteenth century are to be found all over Greece, even though much of the area was under Frankish rule, and building still continued on an extensive scale even after the Turkish conquests of the fifties of the fifteenth century. There are some very delightful churches at Mistra, and though Italian elements are present in some of them, the style of the buildings still remains essentially Byzantine. But the finest, and largest, of the later churches are on Mount Athos, where the monastic communities retained quite a considerable economic prosperity, so that they were able to sponsor work on an extensive scale. The multiple domes on their tall drums, the

Plate 29

arcaded façades, and the semi-domes which were there favoured as terminations for the roofs of the transepts constitute one of the great charms of the Athos monasteries, especially when seen

Plate 31

from the towers or from the windows of rooms built on a higher level, as they often are in the case of monasteries constructed up the slopes of a well-nigh precipitous hill-side. Often the exteriors of these Athonite churches are plastered over and the whole colour-washed in a bright hue.

SECULAR ARCHITECTURE

We know much less about Byzantine secular architecture than we do about the churches, for practically nothing survives, and it is necessary to refer to depictions in mosaics or on ivories to gather some idea of what the early secular buildings were like. Almost the only early secular structure that remains above ground at Constantinople is the so-called 'House of Justinian' above the sea wall; it is probably to be dated to the eighth century. Much of the Great Palace had apparently fallen into ruin by the twelfth century, for excavations have shown that by then parts of it were used as a refuse dump. The emperors had moved to a new palace, the Blachernae, near where the land walls meet the Golden Horn; a part of this palace, known either by the Turkish name of 'Tekfour Serai' or as 'The Palace of Constantine Porphyrogenitus', still survives. Both names are misleading, for it is certainly not Turkish and the presence of the Palaeologue monogram ΠΑ on the walls suggests that much, if not all, the building as it now stands was set up by one of the emperors of that line. It is a comparatively modest structure of three storeys, but its upper rooms, with their large windows, must have been very pleasant. But though it must once have been delightful, it can never have been very magnificent. The west front of the church of St Sophia at Ochrid, dating from 1317, is also of secular rather than ecclesiastical character; it was followed almost exactly in the Fondaco dei Turchi at Venice, and probably reproduces the idea of a palace façade; the palace of Ravenna, as depicted in the mosaics of St Apollinare Nuovo, may be compared.

Plate 25

Plate 27

Plate 30

Plate 26

DEFENSIVE ARCHITECTURE

Plates 1, 2

The defensive architecture of the Byzantine age seems to have been somewhat unambitious beside that of the west or of Islam. The walls of Constantinople, built in the fifth century under Theodosius II, are of course outstanding. They must have been repaired from time to time and the masonry of each age was distinct. Walls of rather similar early date survive in cities like Nicaea; at Trebizond, the fine citadel dates in the main from the thirteenth century. Parts of the walls of such towns as Kaisareh, the ancient Caesarea, are also Byzantine rather than Turkish. But there is nothing very distinctive about these defences, and in the nearer east it was left to Islam to produce such ideas as machicolation, the barbican, the deflected entrance and so on, which were eventually to be brought to the west by the Crusaders and developed as part of the panoply of the age of chivalry. Nor can it be said that the Byzantines gave a great deal to the architecture of castles. True, defensive castles were built in large numbers, especially in the eastern provinces, where their vestiges top numerous hills to this day. But they were usually small in scale and unambitious in plan, and seem to have been erected cheaply, to serve an urgent need, rather than because of any enthusiasm for castles as such, like that which produced such wonderful results in the Gothic world. The character of these castles indeed reflects very clearly the Byzantine outlook, where the military profession was never very highly regarded, and where the word was always believed to be more important than the sword. Only when defence was associated with pomp were truly inspiring architectural results Plate 4 produced, as in the Golden Gate at Constantinople. It is strong and massive, and forms an important part of the defensive system, but it is also a triumphal entrance, and is important as a variant on the Roman triumphal arch rather than as a fortress.

Of Byzantine houses we know practically nothing, though it has been suggested that some of the buildings that survive today on the shores of the Golden Horn, and which are now used as warehouses, are actually to be assigned to late Byzantine times. It is, however, more likely that they were built after the Turkish conquest by Genoese or Venetian merchants, who had their business premises below and their living quarters above. But they no doubt reproduce closely the type of building that existed under the Palaeologues, even if not at an earlier date.

Though they are mostly post-Byzantine – that is to say, date from after 1453 – a word must be said of the monasteries of Plate 28 Athos, for they no doubt give a very good idea of what the great monasteries of Byzantine times must have been like. Even if the defensive character that distinguishes the outsides of the older foundations on Athos was absent in the monasteries that stood in the towns, like the famous monastery of Studios at Constantinople, the interior dispositions were probably well-nigh identical. The hub of the monastery was the church, usually placed in the centre and surrounded by courtyards. There was in all of the monasteries a large refectory, with frescoed walls and with marble-topped D-shaped tables, and there was a library, which on Athos, for reasons of safety from raiders or fire, was housed in a tall square tower. For the rest the monastery consisted in the main of small rooms or cells, built in multiple-storeyed blocks, with open galleries overlooking the court. The cloisters, fraters, dorters and other features which characterised the monasteries of the west were all absent in the Orthodox world, for the monks had small private chambers of their own. Monastic architecture there was thus less monumental than in the west. But the monasteries of Athos have an intimate charm, at times even a fantastic beauty; most astonishing of all is the monastery of Simopetra, which has not unaptly been compared to the Potala Palace at Lhassa.

MONASTERIES

Plate 31

CHAPTER V

Their Life

The Fathers of the Church, by uninterrupted usage, were accustomed to exercise themselves in the learning of the Greeks. This they did with a view to improving and polishing the mind, and at the same time to enable them to refute the errors of the heathen.

SOCRATES, *Historia Ecclesiastica III, c.* 16

INDEPENDENCE OF OUTLOOK

ONE OF THE most outstanding conclusions that emerges from a study of the social history of the Byzantine world is that the people as a whole were surprisingly independent and surprisingly individual. Slaves there were on the great estates in the countryside as well as in the houses of the rich in the towns, and they continued to be employed at least as late as the tenth century. But the population, not only that of the capital, but also that of much of the countryside, seems to have been independent in status and in outlook, both able and ready to express its own will. Indeed, at times it was perhaps all too ready to do so, for the same love of personal independence which characterised classical Greece and characterises modern Greece today seems to have dominated in Byzantine times also, though it was perhaps more controlled and was not permitted to interfere with the course of government to quite so great an extent. Yet public opinion could, and did, remove an emperor or some unpopular government official or court favourite.

Apart from this knowledge of the power of public opinion we do not know a very great deal about the status or the day-to-day life of the people. The slaves appear on the whole to have been well treated, for though slavery was countenanced by the Church, both masters and men were exhorted to respect their mutual obligations, and oppression was severely frowned on. The slaves who were fortunate enough to have good masters were indeed probably better off than the poorer freemen, who in the cities often led difficult, even miserable, lives. The slaves were even permitted to work for others in their free time and could in this way earn money for themselves, and might eventually hope to buy their freedom. How long it was before prisoners taken in battle, who were normally enslaved, could hope to do this it is not possible to say, but it would seem that most of them were fairly rapidly incorporated into the normal population; many were no doubt in due course settled in Asia Minor as peasants with obligations of military service.

THE PEASANTRY

Till the eleventh century, when the power of unscrupulous tax gatherers and rapacious landowners increased, the conditions of the Byzantine peasantry must in general have been preferable to those in most of the remainder of the mediaeval world. Revolts for social reasons practically never occurred, and had there been serious discontent it is hardly likely that the mighty power of Islam would have been so long resisted. Everyday life must have been very similar to that of the Turkish peasant of today. Ploughs drawn by oxen or mules were used, but there was also a good deal of hand work, and double-pointed hoes or mattocks were the favourite tools, though two-pronged forks and spades of normal form were also employed. The usual beast of burden was the donkey or mule, a bundle of goods being strapped on each side of its back; an amusing representation of one, with two bundles of wood, appears among the mosaics of the Great Palace; its owner had apparently climbed on to its back on top of the wood, and the mule is shown in the process of kicking him off. Carts were used also, usually drawn by oxen. Irrigation was perhaps more extensively practised than today, for the population of Asia Minor and the western Balkan lands must have been considerable, and a good deal of grain was also required for the capital. The methods of work employed by other labourers and artisans, such as the stonemason, seem to have been, like the agricultural

Plate 37

Plates 32, 36

Plate 47

Plates 34, 35

ones, the same as those in vogue till very recent times, and the
Plate 33 nature of the flocks or the life of their herdsmen can hardly have changed till most recent times.

It is not easy to present a picture of living conditions, for no private houses have survived from Byzantine times and as yet no city of post-Justinianic date has been thoroughly excavated. The rich must have led an existence similar to that of the upper-class Romans, and their houses were well built and spacious. The better ones had two floors and were built around a courtyard with a blank wall towards the street. The houses of Pompeii, Delos or Ostia no doubt give a fairly clear idea of what they were like. The records tell us that those at Constantinople sometimes had bow-windows through which the ladies
Plate 64 watched events outside. An ivory at Trier depicting the transportation of relics in a four-wheeled cart shows a large building behind with men on the roof and women looking out of the windows in this way. If not properly heated the houses could be very cold, as we learn from the story of the western ambassador Liutprand of Cremona, who was very badly lodged during his embassy to Nicephorus Phocas in 968. What the houses of the poor were like we do not know, though in a document of the fourth century there is mention of basement rooms; it was stated that those living in them were more susceptible to the plague than others because of the staleness of the air. It does not sound as if this accommodation was of very high quality. But there was a considerable and reasonably prosperous artisan class in the towns, and they may well have been rather better off.

The great country estates of the eleventh century, where members of the aristocratic families often spent the summers, or to which they retired if exiled for religious or political reasons, must have been on a considerable scale, with workshops and room for numerous attendants attached to them. One of the larger Roman villas of the third century probably serves to give a good idea of their character. The description of the household of the widow Danielis in the ninth century gives a hint of their size and luxury; she seems to have owned a great portion of the Peloponnese, and she left to the emperor Basil I, whose close friend she was, nearly three thousand slaves.

GUILDS

Artisans were all organised into guilds and corporations. Every industry formed a corporation, and of these many were subdivided into several guilds. There were as many as five in the silk industry. First was that of the men who bought the raw materials, then that of the spinners and weavers, then that of the dyers, then that of those who distributed the finished article, and finally that of the merchants who dealt in imported, as distinct from home-manufactured, silks. Conditions of admission to the guilds, profits, and to some extent wages also were all controlled by the state. The son of a guild member had in most cases to follow his father's calling, and it was very difficult to change from one profession to another. All this must have resulted in a good deal of lack of freedom, but it also assured reasonably fair treatment and regular employment, and was responsible for maintaining a high standard of quality.

Plate 50

COSTUME

Plate 32

The various classes in society were distinguished one from another by their clothes. Workmen wore short tunics reaching to the knees; the upper classes had similar tunics, but they were longer and, of course, of better material. The toga had fallen out of fashion and was worn only on ceremonial occasions, rather like the tail coat now. The poor usually went barefoot; the rich wore sandals or soft leather boots reaching to the calf. Most men were clean shaven, though priests wore beards. In Justinian's time beards were also usual among the leaders of the circus factions, who wore very extravagant clothes. They must have been rather like the 'Teddy Boys' of today, and like them constituted a rowdy element; trouble constantly emanated from their circle. But quite a few of the emperors were bearded, as we see from their portraits on the coins.

Plate 59, *b*

The official costumes were rich and elaborate. The basis was a long, tight-sleeved tunic of silk, over which was worn the *dalmatic*, with embroidery at the shoulder and foot. Above this, again, came the *pallium*, a long strip of jewelled and embroidered material with a hole at the centre for the head; the back formed a train, which was usually brought to the front and
Plates 38, 39 held over the left arm; we see it worn about 500 by the Empress Ariadne and again, in the tenth century, by Romanus and his queen Eudoxia. Crowns, with pendants at the sides made of bejewelled leather, were also usual, and cloaks sometimes cov-
Plate 41 ered the whole, as in the portraits of Justinian and Theodora in San Vitale at Ravenna. The *pallium* was not always worn, for Nicephorus III Botiniates, as represented in a manuscript in
Plate 93 the Bibliothèque Nationale (Coislin. 79), is without it. Jewelled gloves and slippers too were worn by the emperors and probably also by the court officials on state occasions. Saintly figures were usually depicted in a conventional classical manner, with an *himation* or cloak above a *chiton*, a sort of shirt, but sometimes they too were shown in Byzantine robes, as for instance in the
Plate 42 case of the procession of female saints in St Apollinare Nuovo
Plate 40 at Ravenna. At war the emperors continued to wear costumes of Roman type, with the addition of stockings and high boots adorned with pearls of a rather oriental type.

Fig. 20. Gold ear-ring. Seventh century. Museum of Antiquities, Istanbul

Women wore long, fairly simple robes, with a kerchief-like head-dress ending in a long end which could be used as a scarf. Jewellery was favoured by all. Bracelets were till Iconoclast times usually of gold, and were thick and heavy. Later silver became more usual, and lighter bracelets with repoussé decorations replaced the heavier ones. Necklaces made up of precious stones and either gold or silver, often fashioned into such forms as small fish, were popular but, to judge from the numbers that have survived, the most usual form of adornment was the ear-ring. The earlier ones are usually of gold, half-moon shaped, and with a pierced decoration leaving a pattern which usually depicted two animals or birds confronted, with a cross between them. The half-moon shape seems to have remained popular, with little change, till quite late times. Ear-rings of precious stones in metal mounts or hanging on thin gold chains were also common and formed a part of the imperial panoply down to the end. Enamels or small stones set in gold were also popular, and filigree work was much admired. Gold was always in general use, but silver apparently grew in popularity as gold became rarer, and was used more often than gold after the eleventh century. In the twelfth century ear-rings that take the form of circular plaques with a loop at the top for suspension became usual; they bore pierced or embossed decorations, often of birds with intertwined necks.

Fig. 21. Gold and jewelled ear-ring. Sixth century. Museum of Antiquities, Istanbul

Another factor which a study of history makes clear is that there was in the Byzantine state every opportunity for a member of the lower social classes to rise to the highest position, even to that of Emperor, provided he had the force of character to do so. Many of the emperors were thus of humble birth and reached the throne through their own abilities, usually by way of the army, but sometimes also through the civil service. Other opportunities were similarly open to those of the humblest origins. An outstanding case is that of Theodora, Justinian's empress, who was the daughter of one of the attendants in the Hippodrome, a very lowly and undistinguished position. She

22

23

24

Fig. 22. Ear-ring of gold filigree work. Tenth century. Private collection

Fig. 23. Ear-ring in form of bird. Tenth century. Private collection

Fig. 24. Gold ear-ring, open-work design. Eleventh century. Museum of Antiquities, Istanbul

was possessed of beauty, and, more important, had a first-class brain, and great energy and drive; she was no doubt immensely attractive. Her first rise from circus surroundings was as the mistress of Hecebolius, governor of Pentapolis in Africa. Rumour speaks deprecatingly of other attachments; the only one of consequence was that for Justinian, who was eventually to marry her and make her his empress. Justin, Justinian's uncle and predecessor as emperor, was a bluff peasant from eastern Europe. Basil I, founder of the Macedonian dynasty, was of peasant stock, and many another emperor rose to power through his own energy and ability, and at times, also, through his own unscrupulousness.

These men, of course, were the lucky ones. There were also a great many able men who remained very poor, as we can learn indirectly from the texts. Thus great importance was attached to almsgiving, and the need for it seems to have been widespread. There were poorhouses to which the needy could go, and in the 'Book of Ceremonies' the chiefs of hospices for the poor and of hostels for the elderly are mentioned along with other court officials. There also seems to have been something in the nature of a health service, the physicians being paid by the government, and there were free hospitals supported both by the government and the Church. But the evidence suggests that medical knowledge was not very advanced, and greater reliance was no doubt placed on faith healing and the miraculous than on anything that could be termed a scientific approach.

CLASS SYSTEM

Though life in the highest circles was accessible to those with sufficient determination, there was none the less a fairly rigid class system, the barriers of which it was probably easier to break down in public than in private life. The idea of a patrician society had been adopted from Rome, and it had been opened up to all men of distinction by Justinian. With the years, titles and dignities were multiplied and at the same time cheapened, so that new titles were introduced at the top, for a rigid hierarchy was always maintained. Court etiquette depended very much on these titles, but outside that circle there was an upper class, a cultured aristocracy, which became very influential in the days of Justinian. The richer men collected round them circles of dependants composed of poorer relatives, men of learning, monks and so on, and these patrons of cultivated life survived in the capital till the end.

EDUCATION

The education available to men of this class was based on the Greek classics and especially on Homer, and it would seem that even an averagely well-educated man was familiar at least with the classical myths and stories. Anna Comnena was intimately acquainted with the classics, and in the eleventh century it sufficed for a courtier to quote two words from Homer οὐ νέμεσις (it were no shame), to express his approval when the emperor brought out his Caucasian mistress, an act which had provoked considerable opposition. The two words sufficed to conjure up the picture of the men of Troy who, gazing on the radiant beauty of Helen, had said, 'It were no shame to fight for such as she'.

To the study of literature was added that of grammar and rhetoric, and, at a more advanced stage, of philosophy and for specialists, of law. Particular attention seems also to have been accorded to Plato and to the writings of the neo-Platonists, but the philosophical studies lacked the clarity and precision of those of ancient Greece, and a mystic, imaginative conception had come to the fore in this field by the eleventh century, when men like Michael Psellos, though approaching their problems from a secular standpoint, were also concerned with matters partly theological, such as the degree of divinity in man. He and his later disciples, men like Michael Italicus and George Arcopolites, based their theorising on the third-century writer Plotinus, who had recommended the thinker to perfect his character by self-observation and self-criticism, but their approach was closer to the mystic conception of the ideal associated with the oriental religions than it was to the philosophy of Plato.

Technical, as opposed to philosophical, learning was not highly valued as an academic subject; it was studied where necessary, as in architecture, by means of the apprentice system, and there seems to have been a well-established practical education of secular character. That technology in itself was fairly advanced is supported by the evidence of the arts, especially architecture, as well as by a charming story relating to Anthemius of Tralles, the builder of Haghia Sophia. Anthemius was at enmity with Zeno, who inhabited the house above his own, and in order to alarm him, collected a series of large cauldrons, putting covers over them, and connecting them with pipes. The water in the cauldrons was then made to boil and the steam, confined to the pipes, shook the building to such an extent that the unfortunate Zeno was terrified, and he and his friends rushed out in alarm thinking that an earthquake was taking place. Anthemius had thus, though he did not know it, discovered the principle of the steam engine many centuries before James Watt.

Primary education seems to have been available for a very wide group of people, both of the middle and of the upper classes, and schools were provided in the country as well as in the towns. In the country, however, education does not seem to have been very well organised. What is surprising is that it was available at all. In theory it began at between six and eight years of age in local schools, where reading and writing formed the main branch of learning. The pupil then passed on, at ten or twelve, to a more advanced institution where classical literature was studied intensively. Up till the time of Justinian both Latin and Greek were taught; after that Latin fell out of general use, though a knowledge of it had to be acquired by specialists like lawyers. At between sixteen and twenty the student then passed on to the university, to practise rhetoric and learn philosophy or law. The mistake was that there greater stress was laid on how a thing was said rather than on its content, so that rhetoric often came to be more highly valued than sound thought. Some of these schools and places of higher learning were attached to the monasteries and at Constantinople one was supported by the Patriarchate, but in general they were secular and the Church was more concerned with the contemplative side of religious life than with learning. But there were learned ecclesiastics nevertheless; Photius, who was no doubt something of an exception, was equally familiar with the classics and the Bible and is said to have had as many as 16,000 quotations at his command. His eighteen sermons certainly give evidence of his very wide and diverse learning, though they are at the same time very straightforward and practical; he laments, for example, the fact that prayers and good deeds are so often confined to times of stress. The teachers and professors were paid by the emperor or by the state except in the case of some of the primary schools, which were of a private character, and parents seem to have been ready to make considerable sacrifices to educate their children.

THE LANDOWNING ARISTOCRACY

Though the educated and cultured élite continued to flourish down to the end, it ceded influence after the eleventh century to the landowning aristocracy. This class seems to have undergone certain vicissitudes. It was important in early times, but with the introduction of the *theme* system became less important and a new class of proprietors on a larger scale than the peasants, but not of aristocratic lineage, grew up. Some indication of the wealth of this class is given in the account of an eighth-century landowner who was not of the aristocracy. He possessed 100 yoke of oxen, 500 grazing cattle, 80 horses and 12,000 sheep. The number of landowners of both types, peasants and yeomen, if one may call them so, declined with the eleventh century, when the power of the large-scale aristocratic landowners began to increase. These people bought up the land of the smaller proprietors, especially at times of stress, when the smaller men were ready to accept virtual serfdom in return for freedom from the tax collectors. The new landowners soon became strong enough even to defy the government. Basil II suppressed a revolt by this group, and other emperors passed laws to limit their power. But with the weakening of the emperors when the Macedonian dynasty ended, the way was left open to them, and the emperors of the Comnene and Ducas lines were both drawn from the landowning class. Before Iconoclasm the landowning families were more numerous but less powerful, and it was rarely that an emperor had been drawn from their ranks.

THE MIDDLE CLASS

Diehl has shown that there was also an important middle class living in the main straightforward, fairly simple lives. He cites as typical Theodota, mother of Michael Psellos, in the eleventh century, and Theoctista, mother of Theodore of the Studios monastery, in the middle of the eighth. The first named, wife of a man of good family but slender means, was taught the feminine accomplishments of a Victorian lady, embroidery, weaving, good housekeeping. She was deeply pious and loved to succour the poor. At her daughter's death she entered a nunnery, and when her husband died soon after, she actually took the veil. Theoctista was more of a blue-stocking, for though she was equally skilled as a housekeeper, she studied in the evenings in order the better to educate her children. She too eventually took the veil, doing so with great vehemence, for she first relinquished her children and then adopted a régime of severe asceticism. There must have been many more like them, though it was the ambitious and the schemers who most often left their names to history.

One of the most unusual things about these ordinary Byzantine men and women was the readiness with which they turned to the religious life and often, indeed, to extremes of asceticism. Nothing was more normal than for a man to enter a monastery or a woman a nunnery, and even if at times the action was the result of political pressure, more often than not it was due to deep religious conviction. And such was the power of religious thought in the Byzantine world that the man or woman turned monk or nun often went to great extremes of self-mortification or bigotry. To show disregard for the body was always accounted a merit, while any tendency towards heresy was a blemish which had to be eradicated, even if the most severe measures were necessary.

RELAXATIONS AND SPORTS

Needless to say there were numerous forms of relaxation. The Hippodrome was a meeting place as well as an arena. The games and races held there were always extremely popular. Seats were free and as many as 40,000 people could be accommodated at Constantinople. Hippodrome games continued in favour till the twelfth century, though the more violent sports practised in Rome were dropped from the programme by Justinian's time. The most popular events were the chariot races, the charioteers being glorified as heroes; on occasions some of the emperors even conducted the chariots themselves. The chariots were frequently depicted in art, especially on silks, where the four-horse chariot, shown frontally, was a favourite

Plates 44, 45

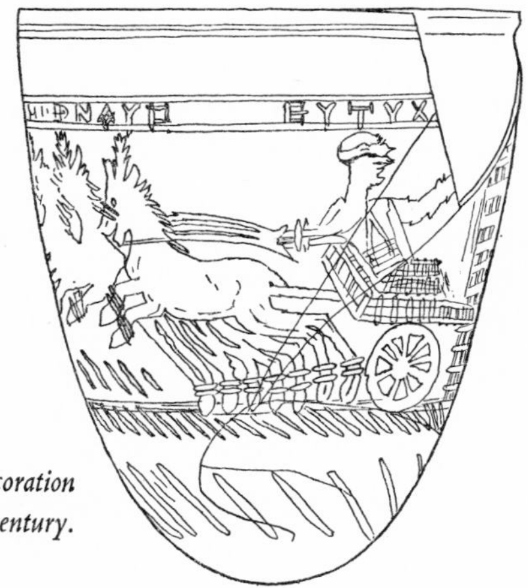

Fig. 25. Glass vessel, bearing decoration depicting a chariot race. Egypt. Fifth century. Stora Collection

motif. There is also an attractive rendering of one on an early
Fig. 25 piece of glass. The spectators, both with regard to the games and the races, were divided into factions, much as are the supporters of football teams today. Originally there were four, but by Justinian's day the number had been reduced to two, known
Plate 43 as the 'Blues' and the 'Greens', and their role had become political, in that each faction not only supported its own team, but also sometimes a rival claimant to the throne or a distinct policy of government. In addition to the normal circus displays, which were the delight of the people, the rich played a sort of polo, before large numbers of spectators; it was called *Tsykanion*, and there were grounds in most of the towns. Tournaments in the western manner were also favoured by the pro-western emperor Manuel II.

Plates 46, 48 Hunting was a popular sport and one emperor, Manuel I, was so keen on it that he moved his residence from the Great Palace to near the walls so that he should not have to ride all the way through the city. Hunting scenes formed a common motif in the floor mosaics of secular buildings, and animals also appear frequently as decorative motifs in the manuscripts. Spears and bows and arrows were the normal weapons of the hunter, and dogs seem to have been regularly used. Some fine
Fig. 26 hunting horns have also been preserved.

Fig. 26. Ivory hunting horn. Ninth century. Kunsthistorisches Museum, Vienna. The ivory bears a Latin inscription not included in this figure, which must have been added at a later date.

Of more static amusements the most popular was furnished by the baths which served as public meeting places, like the pump rooms at a Spa, as well as for the necessary factor of washing. More official in character were theatrical performances, though practically nothing in the way of secular drama has *Fig. 27*

Fig. 27. Byzantine bath, as depicted on an ivory of the Forty Martyrs at Berlin. Probably twelfth century

come down to us. Religious plays, like the drama Christos Pascon, were popular and miracle plays were also performed. It has been suggested that the architectural backgrounds that play so important a part in the later frescoes were modelled on the scenic backgrounds not only of the Hellenistic but also of the Byzantine theatre, and certain of the vivid scenes that we see in the wall paintings of Macedonia and Serbia from the thirteenth century onwards would also appear to reflect dramatic spectacles. Radojčić even suggests that the scene of the Mocking of Christ at Staro Nagoričino, where children dance in the foreground, is to be regarded as a parody of the ballets danced before the emperor at court ceremonies, and other dancing scenes may be representational rather than purely illustrative, as for example in the illustration to Psalm 150 at Lesnovo (1341–1349). Children seem to have played quite a prominent part in the dramatic world, but there are few records regarding the role of women, except for the tradition that Theodora had been a dancer. Plate 49

POSITION OF WOMEN

In everyday life, on the other hand, women had a very active part to play. True, they had their own quarters in the houses and special places in the churches and that at times they went veiled is suggested by the fact that Psellos, at the middle of the eleventh century, records that his mother ventured to lift her veil, careless of whether men saw her or not, because of her great grief at her daughter's death. But otherwise they moved freely in society and their rights with regard to property were the same as those of men. They could act as guardians of minors, and in divorce their interests were considered equally with those of their husbands. They could, and often did, become extremely learned, and on occasions managed their country estates with great efficiency. Their general position is probably accurately reflected by the number of women who ruled as powerful regents or even in their own right as empresses. But the empresses could not, of course, perform one of the most importent of the imperial duties, that of commanding at war, and Michael I Rhangabe (811–813) gave rise to considerable ill feeling in the army by taking his wife Procopia with him on a campaign against the Bulgars.

The Byzantines were, however, never a very warlike people. St Basil had decreed that a soldier who killed should do three years' penance, and though this dictum was soon discarded, the soldier's profession was never a favoured one, nor was death in battle ever considered glorious. Even to fight against the infidel was to be avoided if possible, and the idea of a religious crusade was something quite foreign to the Byzantine outlook. The endless intrigues and quibbles of Byzantine diplomacy which have so shocked westerners were often enough the outcome of a genuine desire to avoid bloodshed, and they come as the natural corollary of the Byzantine attitude towards military action. As a consequence a competent and highly organised diplomatic service was considered almost as important as the army. Yet the maintenance of a strong army was an ever-present necessity, and even if they could hardly compare in efficiency with the Roman, the Byzantine military forces were seldom negligible and often of outstanding quality.

MILITARY ORGANISATION

The legionary system had ceased to exist before Justinian's day. In his time, which is really the first phase of military significance that can be termed Byzantine, a new organisation had been devised. The army was divided into two commands, a static force of men settled in each region, who gave up only part of their time to military duties, and a mobile field force which even in Justinian's day was partly of a mercenary character. The best troops were drawn from Illyria, Thrace and Isauria; the mercenaries were Huns or Herulians and later Langobardians, who served as cavalry. They were valuable as scouts, but less reliable than the regular cavalry, of which there were two types, the light cavalry known as *foederati* and the heavy cavalry from Asia Minor, known as *cataphracti*. In addition certain of the generals had their own private 'guards' regiments which were well trained and highly reliable, though only in so far as their own general was concerned. Belisarius' private guard numbered some seven thousand. They were in some degree modelled on the *comitati* of the northern kings, and were armed with bows as well as swords. In the ninth century four regiments of imperial guards were also recruited and equipped as cavalry, and there were some regiments of foot guards as well. The heavy foot soldiers normally used spears, and carried swords, and usually shields also. The more important men wore chain mail; portraits of emperors, like that of Basil II at the beginning of his psalter at Venice, or representations of the Warrior Saints, like St Theodore, serve to give an idea of their appearance. The cavalry used spears and battle axes. But perhaps the most important weapon was the bow, and it was to the skilful employment of their archers that many of the Byzantine generals owed their victories. The introduction of the bow as a standard weapon was a very important move,

Plate 40

Plate 51

for it gave a new flexibility to the otherwise rather cumbersome forces, and it played a considerable role in bringing about Belisarius' victories; time and again it was the mass of accurate arrow shots that routed an enemy before he was able to establish contact. At a later date the famous Greek fire achieved similar results, especially in naval battles, and as time went on it was the superiority of equipment more than the actual quality of the troops that brought about Byzantine victories.

As a result of the loss of Syria and Palestine to the Arabs in the seventh century the whole defensive system was reorganised, and it was then that the idea of settling a residential territorial force along the frontiers of Asia Minor was most fully developed. The normal unit of administration was the band, of about 350 men. The number of bands in a particular formation fluctuated; it was indeed never constant, so that it would be made more difficult for an enemy to estimate the strength of his opponent. But at no time were the military forces very large. Belisarius conquered Africa with some 15,000 men and in the tenth century the whole army numbered little more than 140,000.

Service in the armed forces was in early days obligatory, though veterans were rewarded with grants of lands in Asia Minor, and it was the conquest of this area by the Seljuks in the eleventh century that led to the most serious weakening of the defensive system. After that time taxes were levied in lieu of service, which weakened both the size and the character of the army, for service could be avoided and individuals who were basically untrustworthy were paid to take the place of the proper conscripts. Manuel I Comnenus made things even worse when he appropriated to the general funds of the treasury taxes intended for the upkeep of the armed forces. From that time onwards the Byzantines had to depend almost entirely on the services of a mercenary army, which was on the whole much less reliable even if it did contain soldiers of very high quality, like the famous Varangian guard.

Though the tasks which confronted the army were unremitting throughout the long period of Byzantine history, the fleet played an equally vital role. The Byzantines were virtually in complete control of the sea until shortly before 700, when Moslem forces began to contest their supremacy. The Moslem fleet was at this time principally manned by Syrians, many of them Christians, but adhering to the Monophysite heresy, and hence ready to serve a Moslem master. It was to a great extent thanks to their skill and dexterity that Constantinople was reached in 670.

But though the Moslems gained ground in the southern Mediterranean, the Byzantines did not relinquish their hold in the north, and the navy helped to save Constantinople at the time of the Arab assault of 718; the Black Sea was always regarded as a Greek preserve. With the transference of the Caliphate from Damascus to Mesopotamia and the establishment of the Abbasid dynasty, the role of Syria became less important, and in consequence the Byzantine fleet was allowed to run down. The results were fatal, for the Moslems captured Crete about 825, and this not only put a valuable strategic centre into their hands, but also provided a base for Moslem pirates, who constituted a threat to commercial shipping in the area for many years to come. The navy was, however, reorganised later in the ninth century, Crete was recaptured in 961, and from then on the situation improved. The expansion of Byzantine power in the west that followed was to no small extent due to the fleet's efficiency. With a strong navy to guarantee safety to shipping, a large commercial fleet grew up also. By the mid-eleventh century Byzantine merchant shipping had captured the trade not only of the northern but also of much of the eastern and southern Mediterranean, and in 1047 Nasr i Khosrau noted that Syria was in fear of a Byzantine attack by sea; Constantine VII had boasted legitimately that he controlled the whole Mediterranean as far as Gibraltar. As the eleventh century went on, the unstable financial position of the central government began to exercise an effect, and Byzantine naval power gradually ceded place to that of the Latins, first to the Amalfitans and then to the Venetians and the Genoese.

Plate 52

Byzantine artists never seem to have mastered the problem of depicting boats of any size, and the records of them in art are wholly conventionalised; more exact information is likely to be provided by the new science of under-water archaeology, for wrecks have recently been examined with most interesting results. It would seem that, even if they were small, the vessels were very seaworthy and manoeuvrable and the successes of the Byzantine navy were to some extent due to good seamanship, but the famous Greek fire was also important. It was the principal offensive weapon and for long remained a secret cherished only by the Byzantines.

TRADE

With the sea routes clear and the land routes of the whole central area under Constantinople's control, as they were until the arrival of the Seljuks in the eleventh century, it is not surprising that trade formed a very essential factor in Byzantine economy. Even at the time of Justinian overseas trade was important, especially with the east, and Cosmas Indicopleustes, a retired sailor, wrote a most interesting account of his journeys to the Malabar coast about 522. Spices, perfumes, ivory and other luxuries came from India; silk, both raw and woven, from China; and jewels and precious stones from Persia. Syria and Asia Minor were sources of cotton and sugar, Asia Minor of the meat supply and metals, while grain came from these provinces and from Egypt. Constantinople was not only the main consumer but was also an important centre of re-export trade. From about 800 onwards, when civilised life began to develop in the west, a good deal of the material that arrived in Constantinople was passed on, and the profits so made constituted one of the main sources of Byzantine wealth. The demands of the capital, with its half a million or more inhabitants, must have been very considerable. In court circles and among the wealthy there was a great desire for luxuries, more especially silk, ivory and precious stones and metals, while among the poorer classes there was a large consumption of necessities, more especially wheat. As the city grew the direction of a large wheat supply thither was essential. In the time of Justinian most of it came from Egypt, and grain of various qualities was available, the finer sorts being used to make bread for the richer classes, while the worse were destined for the poor.

With the Islamic conquest of the seventh century Egypt ceased to be available as a source of grain supply, but it is probable that for a time at least less corn was needed, for the population of Constantinople seems to have declined after a plague in 542, and by the early eighth century it had become considerably reduced. Other areas such as Sicily and southern Russia were no doubt able to make up any deficiency that existed, and by the mid-ninth century, when the population was increasing, the area around Salonica had begun to export corn. But the imports were only required to supplement the production of Thrace and Asia Minor, which was probably quite considerable. At one time, however, grain from Asia Minor was being shipped across the Black Sea to Russia to satisfy a deficiency; this represented a reversal of the normal course of trade.

The grain trade was originally in the hands of merchants, who increased considerably in numbers and in wealth between the sixth and the tenth centuries in spite of the period of depression and economic recession in the seventh. With the eleventh, much of it passed into the hands of the great landowners, and land transport to some extent superseded that by sea as a result of the decline in Byzantine naval power.

After grain the most important commodities of trade were probably textiles and metals, and trade in these commodities, as indeed in all other things, was closely controlled by the government. Until the time of Justinian all the silk had to be imported. Most of it probably came by way of Egypt, but the land routes were also important, both via Syria and the Persian Gulf, and through Persia. Persia however exacted heavy duties, and a new route to the north, by way of Soghdiana, seems to have become widely used in the last quarter of the sixth century. The silk was brought both woven and as raw material, mainly for the imperial looms at Constantinople, though there were important factories in Syria also. When once the cultivation of silk in the west had begun in Justinian's day, there seems to have been a move to make its manufacture an imperial monopoly. Heraclius issued decrees for the control of factories elsewhere, and soon after his death manufacture seems to have been concentrated at Constantinople, and it continued to be so at any rate till the tenth century; but finished materials were no doubt imported from Syria. Later, in the twelfth century, we read of factories at Thebes and Corinth, and textiles seem to have been woven on some of the great estates also.

The products of the imperial looms were distinguished by their excellence, and the secrets of technique were jealously guarded. The workshops were situated in the palace area, and employment in them was much coveted. Most of the employees were men; it was held that women were less reliable as they might run away and disclose the secrets of manufacture. All the best and finest stuffs were reserved for the emperor and officially never came into the hands of the merchants at all. But there seems to have been a fairly active black-market, and only the purple stuffs were wholly reserved. The strictness of control is well illustrated by the story of the ambassador Liutprand of Cremona, for in 968 the customs seized silks in his possession in spite of the fact that Nicephorus Phocas had given permission for him to take them with him; on a previous visit to the Emperor Constantine VII in 949 similar permission had been given and he had experienced no difficulty. Home demand must have been considerable, for silks were extensively used as hangings in the churches, palaces and houses of the nobles, and all the richer members of society wore costumes of elaborate figured silks, in any case on official occasions. Their richness, even in the last, impoverished, age of the Palaeologues, is indicated by quite a number of portraits of members of the royal family or court dignitaries in their official robes. Plates 92–95

The export of woven silks, other than those from the imperial looms, constituted a very profitable trade all through Byzantine history. The Moslem rulers seem to have been especially valued customers, and received favourable terms, perhaps because so much of the eastern trade was controlled by them. Antioch and Aleppo in the south and Trebizond in the north were the most important entrepôts for this trade. No doubt ivory, spices and so forth were sent from the east in return. The transfer trade over the Syrian route was, however, considerably reduced as a result first of the decline of the Abbasid caliphate in the eleventh century and then because of the Crusades, which disrupted the life of the whole area. The extensive trade which had centred on Baghdad and travelled thence to the west via north Syria, Asia Minor and Constantinople, was transferred to Egypt, and from there it was carried not in Byzantine but in Italian vessels. This was one of the causes that contributed to the rise of Italian and the gradual decline of Byzantine shipping, and which made it possible for the Italian merchants to demand such favourable concessions in the Byzantine world. Similarly, the weakening of the Abbasids opened the way for the expansion of the Turks and the eventual conquest of Asia Minor by the Seljuks. Once they were in possession of Asia Minor there is reason to believe that trading relationships were established between the Seljuks and the Byzantines, and the Seljuk port of Adalia became one of the main trading centres in the east Mediterranean. It is a point which careful investigation of Seljuk and later Byzantine sites should be able to clarify.

Privileges in the silk trade were in the great middle period also granted to the Bulgars, in return for imports such as linen and sugar, and there was a regular trade with Russia across the Black Sea. It had extended up the Dniepr and even as far as the Baltic at least by the time of Rurik in the second half of the ninth century. Furs, honey, wax and slaves were offered in return for Byzantine goods. The value and quality of the silks that could be sent to Russia was, however, limited by law. The most favoured items of export were probably gold and silver brocades, but other things went also, and excavations at Cherson in sites of the tenth and eleventh centuries have produced pottery of Byzantine type, some of which was undoubtedly exported from Constantinople. Conversely, at a rather later date, pottery made in the Chersonese found its way to Black Sea ports in Asia Minor; examples have been found at Trebizond and Samsun.

Trade in silks with the Latin west was perhaps never quite as important as that with the east and north, though until the Italians learnt to make such things the east was the main source of supply, and it is thanks to their preservation in western treasuries that we know the best Byzantine silks. They were used there for the burial of saints, bishops and kings, and also as book ends, sealbags and so forth; these must represent the residue of larger textiles which had been employed as hangings, costumes or vestments and then become worn out.

Plates 65–67

The export of certain other commodities was forbidden, in addition to that of the silks from the imperial looms. Gold could thus only leave the empire for official reasons; salt fish, which formed the staple diet of the populace, could not be exported, and certain raw materials which were needed at home were also reserved. Lending at interest was forbidden by law except in certain particular instances intended to foster trade. The exports of metal goods were on the other hand probably considerable, though we know less about this trade than we do about silk. Constantinople was the main centre for fine metalwork, in any case after the seventh century, when Antioch and Alexandria fell to the Moslems, for the industry was concentrated there by design, and work done elsewhere was provincial in style. Many of the silver dishes that are among the most important Byzantine products of the early age bear stamps or hallmarks, and technical study has shown that these must have been put on after the decorations were done, so that the dishes must have been made in the imperial workshops and not merely stamped there. The carving of ivories and precious stones must also have been centred in the main on Constantinople, for the style of the capital is quite clear and obvious, and once again provincial works can be easily distinguished.

We know that in early times the silver vessels formed an important commodity of exchange; the numerous examples found as far afield as Russia and Britain prove this. But after the tenth century there is not very much evidence to suggest that finished metal objects were extensively exported. The numerous Byzantine objects that are preserved in cathedral treasuries in the west mostly came there as loot after the fourth crusade rather than as purchases or gifts at an earlier date. Previously the silver vessels had probably often been used as payments to assure the tranquillity of barbarian tribes, in accordance with established Byzantine custom. After the seventh century, if such payments were made they were doubtless in actual coin, and the esteem in which the 'bezant' was held attests the value set upon the coinage. Ostrogorsky has indeed shown that after the ninth century Byzantine economy was essentially a monetary one. The salaries of officials, the pay of the army, the wages of the labourers, even fines, were all paid in coin, and loans granted to merchants and shipowners by the treasury were apparently in coin also. The monetary system was in fact more highly developed in the mid-Byzantine period than at any previous time.

Plates 53–56

FISCAL PROBLEMS

The expenses of the state must have been enormous. Defence was always a primary matter, and costs were high even at times when the army and navy were neglected. Indeed, pay for all the services seems to have been on a generous scale, and the higher ranking officers of the army and the civil servants received very large salaries. The administration, though apparently efficient, was large and ponderous and officials were legion. They received food and clothing as well as cash payments for their services. There were numerous charitable institutions to keep up, and the expenses of the court were especially high, for it was maintained on a lavish, wholly oriental scale even in the impoverished days of the twelfth century. The upkeep of the capital itself, with its numerous public buildings and some twenty kilometres of walls, including those along the sea fronts as well as the land walls, must have entailed a very heavy drain on the resources. And finally, and perhaps almost most expensive of all, there was the need for gold to implement the Byzantine policy of buying peace rather than fighting.

The revenue to meet these costs was raised in a number of ways. A large income was obtained from the property owned by the state. It consisted firstly of agricultural land, and though much was given away as a reward for military and other services, much was also acquired, especially in the middle period when the lands of many of the powerful were confiscated as a penalty for the part they played in revolts against the legitimate government. Secondly the government owned a good deal of urban property, which brought in a considerable revenue. It consisted of houses and of large bonded warehouses which were rented out to merchants and traders. Then the state controlled a good many of the industries, and if some of these, like that of armaments, perhaps did not bring in very much, they nevertheless saved a lot of expenditure. Mines and quarries were also a state monopoly. And finally, and most important, was the monetary taxation. Most profitable were the customs dues of ten per cent on all imports and exports and the taxes on agricultural land, which comprised charges on grazing, as opposed to working, cattle and on the various holdings in each village. In collecting these the village was regarded as the fiscal unit, not the individual, and if one man defaulted his neighbours had to pay. There was also a capitation tax on serf households, and there were a number of taxes on the urban population which were intended to equalise the burden of the rural land tax. These comprised taxes on consumer goods, an inheritance tax, and fees for licences to follow certain callings. It would seem, however, that a heavier burden fell on the agriculturalists than on the town dwellers. There were also occasional, non-recurrent, levies for special purposes. On the whole taxation until the twelfth century seems to have been fair and reasonable; only then did the collectors, seeing the weakness of the central government, begin to feather their own nests. Or, with the *pronoia* system, where lands were granted to the wealthy for life, the holders sometimes extorted all they could from the unfortunate peasants.

The economy of Byzantine times knew periods of recession and expansion, just as in the modern world. For example the seventh and earlier eighth centuries saw a period of recession, and there was an age of great expansion under Theophilus between 829 and 842. But on the whole the level seems to have been remarkably stable, and Byzantine coinage maintained its value as a world trading unit from the time of Constantine I to that of Michael IV (1034–1041), when it was for the first time seriously debased, with very unhappy results. Though stabilised by the thrift of the Nicaean emperors between 1204 and 1261, the Byzantine coinage at Constantinople never wholly regained its value or its former influence as an international medium, and after 1261 it was really beyond the power of the small empire that the Byzantine had become to support the great capital city whose trade was by then almost entirely in the hands of foreigners, who enjoyed considerable privileges and were almost entirely exempt from taxation.

CHAPTER VI

Their Faith

There are two main gifts bestowed by God upon men: the priesthood and the imperial authority. Of these the former is concerned with things divine, the latter with human affairs. Proceeding from the same source, both adorn human life. Nothing is of greater importance to the emperors than to support the dignity of the priesthood so that the priests may in their turn pray to God for them.

JUSTINIAN, *Sixth Novella*

IMPORTANCE OF RELIGION

IN NO STATE, with the possible exception of Ancient Egypt, did religion play a more essential part in determining not only the nature of the people's lives but also the course of history than in the Byzantine. In no state did the affairs of the Church or the business of the dogmatic theologian enter so universally into the life and thought of the people as a whole. Yet, if in the one direction the nature of the official faith very seriously affected life and at times also political events, on the other the past history of the area also exercised an important influence on the way in which the faith itself developed. Indeed, it was to a great extent the influence of the locality that was responsible for making Byzantine Christianity (and with it the faith of the Orthodox world) distinct from Roman Christianity (and with it the faith of Roman Catholicism). It is, indeed, hard to believe that the two Churches, the eastern and the western, would, or could, ever have reached complete agreement, quite apart from the various events, political and theological, that eventually brought about the final separation in the eleventh century.

True, eastern Christianity, as sponsored by the earlier Byzantine emperors, had a great deal in common with that of Rome. The Fathers of the Church in both areas were faced with the problem of eradicating paganism, yet in both areas a good many pagan ideas were assimilated. Certain ceremonies of the Church owed not a little to the ritual of pagan Rome; quite a number of pagan elements from the eastern religions were incorporated into the Church's teaching; a belief in not a few classical myths lived on at least till the ninth century, for we find them being inveighed against by Photius in his ninth homily. In some ways the mystic religions of the East had prepared the ground for Christian teaching, yet in others this proved an even greater danger than classical paganism, because of the close similarity of many of their tenets to those of early Christianity. These beliefs had made some headway in Italy, but their legacy was far more profound in the east, for the mystic, transcendental outlook that was to distinguish the faith of the Byzantine world was to a great extent derived from them.

It was thus to a very mixed society that the Church preached under the earlier Christian emperors, and it was to a great extent because of this that the problem of definitions appeared so important and the dangers of heresy so considerable and so ever present. Needless to say, in a society which loved argument and rejoiced in hair-splitting detail, the definitions presented endless scope for disagreement, and as the decisions of the early Councils of the Church were intended to be universal, those who did not subscribe to them were forthwith denounced as heretics. That they mostly carried with them large sections of the Christian community did not in any way deter those whose beliefs were not identical, and who had lost sight of the simple faith taught by Christ.

The Armenians, who had adopted Christianity as their official religion about 280, and the Georgians, who were converted in the early fourth century, were not involved in the disputes, for their territories fell outside the empire. The principal actors in the drama were the Bishops from Italy, Egypt, Syria and the Byzantine area, with the patriarchs of Rome, Alexandria, Antioch and Constantinople as the protagonists.

COUNCILS OF THE CHURCH: HERESIES

The first Council assembled at Nicaea in 325 to discuss the Arian heresy. Arius, a learned and influential teacher, had argued that if the Father begat the Son there must have been a time when the Son did not exist, and he therefore placed the Son in a position below that of the Father. His teaching took a considerable hold, but was argued against with the greatest force, and at the Council agreement was reached that the two were of like nature, the word *homoousios*, 'of the same substance', being adopted to define their relative positions. The teaching of Arius was condemned, and he was declared a heretic, though the heresy survived at least till Justinian's time and some of the great churches of Ravenna were set up by Arians, notably the baptistry which is still known by that name.

The use of the word *homoousios* was given further sanction at the second Council, held at Constantinople in 381, when the creed which we know today as the Nicene was also finally approved; it had first been propounded at Nicaea in 325. The position of the Patriarch of Constantinople was determined at the Council, for the city was assigned second place after Rome. The elevation of Constantinople above Antioch, and more especially above Alexandria, was not well received by the clerics from those places; it was perhaps to some extent responsible for the spread, later, of Monophysitism in Egypt.

The third Council, held at Ephesus in 431, was mainly concerned with a discussion of Nestorianism. According to the teaching of Nestorius, leader of the Antioch school, the human aspect of Christ's nature was to be regarded as of paramount importance. He was opposed by the Alexandrines, who regarded Christ primarily as the incarnate Logos, and stressed His divine aspect. The Alexandrine view carried the day, and Nestorius was declared a heretic, in spite of the fact that he had the Emperor's support. This involved the breakaway of a very large section of the Church in the east which was, later, to extend as far as China and which at one moment almost claimed the Mongol empire in its sway.

The fourth Council was called at Chalcedon in 451, and again centred around the discussion over the two natures of Christ. Agreement was finally reached to describe them as united without absorption, without admixture, without division and without separation. Both Nestorius and the Monophysites were condemned, for the latter held that Christ had but one nature, at once divine and human. It was as a result of the findings of Chalcedon that Egypt broke away, and that the Coptic Church was eventually established as a separate entity.

The fifth Council, at Constantinople in 553, was really summoned by Justinian for political rather than theological reasons, to try to reach a decision which would unite the Orthodox centre, the Monophysite south, and the Nestorian east. Agreement was reached with regard to the condemnation of certain writings, but it proved impossible to reconcile the divergent views of the experts, even with imperial persuasion, and Christian doctrine as it had been formulated at the Council of Chalcedon was ultimately accepted by the Churches of Constantinople and Rome and their numerous adherents. This was the last of what may be termed the fundamental Councils, where the basic essence of the conception of Christ was discussed. But other heresies were to arise, such as that of the Monothilites, according to which the divine and human natures of Christ were regarded as united in a single active force. This seemed to offer a compromise between the dogma of Chalcedon and the heresy of the Monophysites, but it was condemned by the sixth Council held at Constantinople in 680, though adherents to the belief still survive to this day in Syria; they are known as the Maronites. The seventh Council held at Nicaea in 751 was concerned with Iconoclasm, and its findings were alternately abjured and ratified in a series of subsequent Synods till the return of the Iconodules in 843.

The numerous Councils that were called in the early centuries of Constantinople's existence to deliberate on the nature of Christian doctrine serve to illustrate the wide diversity of views, and though the major principles had been formulated and annunciated by the time of Justinian, diversity of opinion on minor matters continued, and as late as the ninth century, when Photius preached his famous sermon in Haghia Sophia on March 29th, 868, before the Emperors Michael III and Basil I, he made reference to the reception into the true Orthodox Church of a band of diversionists. These were called Quartodecimans and it appears that members of this sect, together with Arians, Sabbatians, Macedonians, Novatians and Apollinarians, were numerous. They were not required to be re-baptised but merely to be anointed with holy oil on their return to Orthodoxy. There seem to have been periodic efforts to stamp them out, but measures were never as severe as against the Paulicians, a sect hostile to any ecclesiastical cult, which continued to exist till the tenth century, when its beliefs were revived in Bulgaria as the basis of the Bogomil heresy.

The various sects numbered their keenest adherents among the inhabitants of Asia Minor, and it is not surprising that when Iconoclasm was formulated as a doctrine in the eighth century it too found its most ready adherents there. The peoples of the east sought a simple, straightforward faith defined by clear-cut rules – that is perhaps one reason why Islam was so readily accepted in Syria and Palestine – and the prolix definitions of the Councils and the complicated ceremonies of the Church at Byzantium were foreign to their outlook though they delighted the Greeks of the seaboard. If the Ancient Greek was, as Aristotle said, a political animal, the Byzantine Greek was equally truly an ecclesiastical one.

The depth to which this ecclesiastical outlook had penetrated is well illustrated by the Byzantine attitude towards the emperor. The old Roman conception of apotheosis had to some extent survived and the emperor was supreme ruler, above the law; yet he held this position only as Christ's vice-regent on earth. A throne, with the Gospels open upon it, was set up in the council chamber, and there was a mosaic of Christ immediately above the imperial throne bearing the inscription 'King in Christ', as a perpetual reminder that Christ was the real ruler of the state. The emperor was elected not, as one might expect, on the hereditary principle, but by the free choice of the army and senate and the acclamation of the people; only in Macedonian times did the hereditary principle become important. From the moment of the acclamation the new emperor was ruler; the coronation service did no more than set the seal of the Church on something that was already an established fact. On the one hand the emperor was almost divine; on the other he was appointed by the people. The highest standards of conduct were enjoined upon him; he had to be temperate, considerate and philanthropic, and was required to respect the law in its smallest detail, and he was liable to excommunication by the Church. But it was also realised that he was a man, subject to human frailty, and it was because of this and because of the charity taught by Christ that his failings, often so extreme, were readily excused. The support of the people was given, however, not to his person but to his office and to its sanction through Christ, and the populace was loyal to him only in so far as the two coincided. When once the office had been assumed by another, allegiance was automatically transferred. *'Le roi est mort; vive le roi'* was never truer than in the Byzantine world, even though the former occupant of the throne might have been most foully disposed of by his successor. It is essential to appreciate the position if the Byzantine attitude to the emperor is to be interpreted in a proper light.

Plate 57

Throughout Byzantine history human frailty was readily accepted and condoned, for the Byzantine outlook was charitable. There was, in the Byzantine make-up, little of morality in the western sense, but faith was none the less sincere, none the less profound for that. That faith could move mountains was indeed a text from the scriptures which was taken very literally in everyday life. Time and again in Byzantine history prayer or, more particularly, the intervention of some icon, had seemed to save a critical situation. On no occasion was this more notably so than in the seventh century when the Arabs were advancing against the capital. The Byzantine forces had been defeated in the field and there seemed little to hinder their conquest of Constantinople itself. The icon of the Virgin, traditional protectress of the city, was brought out and paraded round the walls. Constantinople was saved. Today the weather, logistics or human incompetence would be put forward to account for the halt of the Arab armies. To the Byzantines the Virgin's love and the power that she vouchsafed through her icon seemed a sufficient explanation. And this happened on numerous occasions. Thus in 865, when the Russian fleet threatened to attack, an icon of the Virgin was taken down to the sea; a great storm arose and the fleet was dispersed.

BELIEF IN THE MIRACULOUS

Miraculous intervention of this kind was accepted as something normal and of everday occurrence. Indeed, to the Byzantine miraculous help came at times to be regarded almost as a right, and if the icon of some saint failed to provide the expected help it was discarded, and a new icon of a different saint was petitioned. It is essential to acknowledge this outlook not only to understand the basis of Byzantine thought, but also to appreciate the true character of Byzantine history. Historians of the past were so often concerned with the course of major events, such as wars, treaties or political negotiations, that they failed to give due attention to this aspect of the Byzantine background, while those of today tend to stress the importance of social or economic causes or are so preoccupied with the material culture of the age that they have little time to be concerned with the conceptions of thought behind it. In the Byzantine world the material was so closely linked to the spiritual, the event with the idea, that the two aspects cannot be divorced. The problem, 'how did the Byzantines think?', which Norman Baynes was really the first to consider seriously, is one of the most interesting that confronts the mediaeval historian today.

The texts tell us but little in a direct way, for the earlier writers were mostly governed by a marked Roman outlook, and were more interested in practicalities, whilst the later ones were more often than not Church historians, primarily concerned with ecclesiastical happenings. But something of the distinctive Byzantine outlook looms through the works of such men as John the Silentiary, in his descriptions of Haghia Sophia or through the writings of Psellos at a later date, and the explanations that were given for success or failure in wars or the devastations of famine or plague are especially informative. They show us that Byzantine thought was not Roman thought Christianised, nor was it oriental thought westernised. It was, probably, the most distinctive aspect of the fusion of the diverse heritages that lay at the basis of Byzantine culture.

The extremes to which the Byzantine belief in the miraculous power of the icons was carried appear somewhat surprising to us today. To the Iconoclasts they verged on idolatry. And the Iconoclasts, looking back to the Old Testament, where men seem to have inclined to idolatry like drunkards to drink, were determined to check the tendency. Like all ardent reformers they often resorted to the most violent acts of oppression to bring about their ends, but that the movement took the forceful aspect it did, especially during the reigns of Leo III (717–741) and Constantine V (740–775) was perhaps to some extent due to the strength of the opposition which it had to encounter in the regions where the Greeks were most strongly entrenched.

THE ICONOCLAST CONTROVERSY

The arguments on both sides were weighty. The Iconoclast case was based on two main dicta, namely that an icon was to be counted as an idol and that an image of the Saviour, in whatever form, undermined the true doctrine as to the dual nature of Christ, for it could only depict the human form and not the divine aspect. The case for the images was based on the assumption that the icon was not an idol, but pertained of the sanctity of the figure depicted as if it were its reflection, and that it served as an intermediary between the material world and the everyday worshipper on the one hand and the spiritual world and the divine essence on the other. It was argued in numerous writings of a highly philosophical character, those of John of Damascus (*c.* 710–*c.* 750) being foremost among them at the outset and those of Theodore of Studios towards the end of the struggle in the ninth century. The case for Iconoclasm is less well presented in surviving literature, for the writings were in many cases destroyed when the movement was brought to an end; nor do the Iconoclasts seem to have been such able writers as their opponents, for they were practical men rather than philosophers. But they argued their case nevertheless.

It is true that Leo III, the first of the Iconoclast emperors, waited for some years after coming to the throne before he took action, for his reign began in 717, and his first Iconoclast edict was issued in 726. But when he took action it was on his own initiative and the Church Assembly which he convened to enforce his policy in 730 was virtually driven to take action by the emperor. Even the Assembly summoned by Constantine V in 754 to reconfirm the ban was something of a put-up affair, though the emperor's policy was very definite, and he was especially active against the monasteries where the opposition to Iconoclasm centred. There were 338 bishops at the assembly but there were no patriarchs and the pope, still the nominal head of the Church, was not represented. He was, needless to say, strongly opposed to the movement. On this occasion, though the images were condemned, their destruction was forbidden. It was perhaps to show his disapproval of Iconoclast rule that Pope Gregory III started to issue his own coinage and that Pope Paul I announced his election in 757 to Pippin and not to the Byzantine emperor.

The most violent phase of Iconoclasm came to an end with Constantine V's death in 775. Leo IV (775–780) abandoned his predecessor's anti-monastic policy, and the next ruler, Irene, guardian of the young Constantine VI, not only restored the images and granted favours to the icon-loving monks, but also summoned a council to reconsider the question of the images. After a first abortive meeting at Constantinople which was broken up by soldiers of the Iconoclast persuasion, it re-assembled at Nicaea in 787 and passed decrees in favour of the images. Suppression of the monks by Nicephorus I (802–811) and the readoption of a milder Iconoclast policy in the early ninth century was due rather to the Emperor's personal dispute with Theodore of Studios, leader of the monastic, anti-Iconoclast party, than to any deeply rooted religious conviction. The more active Iconoclast policy instituted by Leo V (813–820) was more sincere, but it brought much misery through fear of informers, who seem to have permeated the whole of society much as in the Communist world today. We read that even husband and wife were fearful of discussing the question of Iconoclasm together.

Michael II (820–829), though somewhat eccentric with regard to his religious beliefs, was on the other hand reasonably tolerant towards the Iconodules, who were given complete freedom outside the capital; inside it the situation was complicated owing to the recalcitrant attitude of Theodore of Studios. The next emperor, Theophilus, was a convinced Iconoclast, who had been educated by one of their ablest thinkers, John the Grammarian. He remained under John's influence when the latter became patriarch, in spite of the Iconodule sympathies of the Empress Theodora. But popular enthusiasm for the movement was by now spent; Theophilus' military reverses were attributed to his Iconoclast outlook, just as a century or so earlier Constantine V's military successes had been regarded as the outcome of his sincerity as an Iconoclast. Iconoclasm was finally brought to an end with the accession of Michael III in 843; it was never to see any serious recrudescence. It had been a forceful, and, so far as the future was concerned, a very formative interlude. Had it not been for Iconoclasm, in spite of all its extremes, the faith of the second great period of Byzantine history would never have developed in the way that it did, Byzantine art of the second period would probably never have acquired so transcendental a character, and the relationships between Byzantium and the west might well have taken a different course.

It was thus really after 843 that eastern Christianity took on its most characteristic and fully developed complexion, and then that the essence of the Orthodox outlook, centring on a profound belief in the reality of the unseen world, came to full maturity. In the development of this outlook the Church, as a concrete entity, as a material structure, played a part which was both primary and essential. It was, first, the centre of the religious life of state and community, and as such, in the Orthodox view, it was also the centre of life as a whole. The Great Palace of the emperors thus contained almost as many churches as it did reception halls, council chambers or living rooms, and in Constantine Porphyrogenitus' 'Book of Ceremonies' the churches play a more important role than any of the other buildings. And secondly the structure of the church constituted the setting for an elaborately contrived decoration, its interior being conceived as a microcosm of the greater world without. Like that other world it was made up of a heavenly sphere above and an earthly one below, and its decoration
Fig. 28 attested this disposition. At the summit of the dome, not only the highest place, but also, by its form, the symbol of the heavens, was set the figure of Christ Almighty, looking down

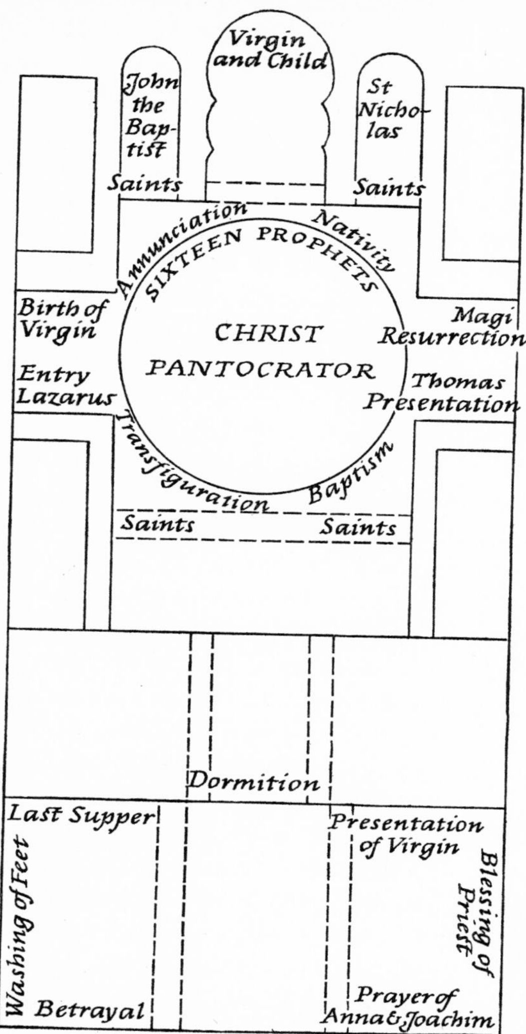

Fig. 28. Daphni, near Athens. Plan to show disposition of the mosaics. c. 1100. After Diez and Demus

on the building as God looked down on the world. In the next most exhalted place, the conch of the apse, was set the Mother of God, and the two divine figures were supported by scenes from their lives, or by their closest associates on earth, the prophets and apostles. The saints were set at a lower level, linking the heavenly sphere with the world below. Similarly the iconostasis or screen, which in later times served to present a closed barrier between the sanctuary and the body of the church, represented the division between the spiritual and the material worlds, and the panel paintings or icons upon it assumed the character of a window opening on to the spiritual sphere. The scheme was first fully developed by Basil I in a church which he founded within the precincts of the Great Palace, called the Nea.

THE HIERARCHY AND THE CHURCH

At the same time the organisation of the Church as an hierarchical institution was developed to a greater degree than previously. At its head stood the patriarch of Constantinople, by Macedonian times already virtually independent of the pope at Rome. The patriarch maintained a very centralised control over archbishops, bishops and clergy throughout Asia Minor and the greater part of the Balkans. He was in the state second only to the emperor and at times was even powerful enough to flaunt the imperial will. Most of the patriarchs were men of learning and piety, though a few were not even ordained until they were appointed. Even if they were sometimes nominated for political reasons, the patriarchs almost always adopted a new outlook when they came to office. This was the case with Tarasius, a layman who was appointed in 784; he turned out to be a patriarch of considerable character and filled the office with great distinction. Even more striking was the case of Photius, certainly the most famous and probably also the most learned of all the patriarchs, who was a layman when he was appointed by Michael III in 858. He was deposed by Leo VI in favour of his own younger brother Stephen, but later returned to office and received the papal recognition which had originally been denied him. Of a rather different character was Theodotus, a married man and a soldier, who was nominated by Leo V; he shocked the faithful by celebrating his election with a great feast, at which fasting priests were compelled to eat flesh. Again, Romanus I appointed his fourth son at the age of sixteen; he was described as a youth more at home in the stables than in the Church. But these were exceptions; all in all the patriarchs were men of ability, character and piety.

The relationship between the patriarch and the emperor was necessarily a very close one. 'When you disagree you bring confusion to the holy churches, and in the world you give rise to no ordinary disturbance,' wrote Daniel the Stylite (409–493) to the Emperor Basiliscus, and the records show that the effects of such disagreement were usually widespread. It is thus not surprising that some of the patriarchs were 'yes' men, but as time went on their power and importance increased, and from the twelfth century onwards it was often the patriarch who gave the final decision in policy rather than the emperor.

The bishops were similarly often actuated by political ends, for many of them came from the upper class and found greater satisfaction in the intrigues of higher office than in the sanctity of religious teaching. They were not permitted to be married, whereas the parish priests could be, so that they were often drawn from monastic circles, and no doubt represented the most active side of monasticism. The monks of the monasteries were never very far removed from hermits and the most pious among them most often sought the solitary life. Monasteries were not usually centres of thought and learning as in the west.

The idea of monastic life was as old, indeed even older, than the Byzantine state, for the faithful had sought refuge as hermits from the earliest times, even before Christianity was recognised, and the idea of self-mortification was from the first associated with that of piety. St Simeon Stylites was by no means the only saint who spent most of his life on the summit of a column, and the greater the extremes of austerity that were resorted to, the greater was believed to be the degree of piety. Thus a certain Theodore of Sykeon was ordained a lector after three years in a cave because the stench of his body and the mass of worms in his hair so impressed a visiting bishop of his sanctity.

MONASTICISM

At first there was no form of monastic organisation; the holy simply sought a solitary life. But the idea of communal effort soon developed, and the first actual monastery was established at Dendereh in Egypt by one Pachomius at much the same time that the new capital was founded by Constantine. Pachomius instituted an organised system where groups of monks had to obey their head or abbot and were also bound to do a certain amount of manual work as a duty. Laurae, or groups of small cells attached to a larger monastery, were founded in Palestine in the fourth century and from there the idea spread to Syria and Asia Minor. Basil of Caesarea, in the fourth century, was, however, the first to organise monasticism as such, and it was he who first stressed the importance of the monastic as opposed to the anchorites' life. He probably left no actual written rules and there was never a Basilian order as there were Benedictine or other orders in the west. But many of the monasteries that were subsequently founded owed a great deal to Basil's teaching, and it was perhaps thanks to ideas stimulated by him that the first mountain monasteries were founded in Bithynia. Subsequently other monasteries were established, the most important being those on Mount Athos. In the east, as for instance in Cappadocia, the communities were usually smaller than in Greece, but one monastery on a larger scale survives to this day, namely that of St Catherine on Mount Sinai. Though all these were monasteries where groups of men associated together, the idea of the solitary hermit continued, and on Athos the hermits were looked upon as particularly holy. When the Lavra was founded there by St Athanasius in 963, only the five most distinguished and pious of the one hundred and twenty original monks were permitted to live as hermits.

At Constantinople itself the first monastery was founded in the reign of Theodosius II, but others were established soon after, and from an early date were granted special favours and throughout practically the whole of Byzantine history they were exempt from taxation. They only began to play a really important role in the affairs of the state as a result of Iconoclasm, partly because the principal opposition to Iconoclasm centred in the monasteries and partly because of the firm line that Theodore, Abbot of the Studios monastery in Constantinople, took against the remarriage of Constantine VI – it was this even more than his opposition to Iconoclasm that led to Theodore's exile and for a time to the suppression of the monastery. Though the monastery had been founded in the fifth century, it seems to have been more or less deserted till Theodore arrived there from the monastery of Saccoudion on Mount Olympus, where he had served as a monk under the famous Abbot St Plato. It was Plato who had introduced a number of new rules into monastic life, including a penitential code and a prohibition not only on the presence of women in monasteries, but also on that of female animals. Plato's rules were further elaborated by Theodore, who insisted that all property should be held in common.

All the early monasteries were cenobitic, that is to say the monks sacrificed all personal property, they took their meals in common, and accepted the authority of their abbot as paramount. Incidentally, they were prohibited from taking more than three baths a year unless they were ill. Only later did the system known as the idiorhythmic come in, which permitted the monks to retain their own property, replaced the authority of the abbot by that of a committee, and put an end to most aspects of the communal life; it was adopted on Athos only in the fifteenth century. Rules were also slackened by the granting of monasteries to laymen, first in Iconoclast times and then in the twelfth century; the laymen sequestered most of the monastic funds, only allowing the monks enough for their bare essentials and preventing the various charitable activities which the monasteries supported, such as the provision of poor houses and hospitals. As early as the tenth century Nicephorus Phocas had denounced the evils that arose from the accumulation of wealth by the monasteries and they played till the end an important role as property owners.

Nunneries seem to have begun as early as the monasteries, but we know much less about them; their rules were similar, and strict poverty and obedience were enjoined, while the day was divided between work and prayer. The nunneries played no political role, nor did they produce much in the sphere of thought or art, with the exception that in later times fine embroideries were made in them. But quite a number of leading women, nobles or even at times deposed empresses or imperial
Plate 58 widows retired to them, just as court officials or emperors retired to the monasteries. In many cases they brought considerable property with them. One of the most interesting was Maria, half-sister of the Emperor Andronicus II Palaeologus, who had been betrothed to Hulagu the Mongol Khan but because of his death married his son Abuka; in her later years she returned to Constantinople and founded the church of St Mary of the Mongols and became a nun under the name of Melane. Her portrait appears below the great mosaic of Christ and the Virgin in Kariye Camii.

The copying of manuscripts, their illustrations, and the production of icons and wall paintings was a normal activity in the monasteries, even if secular copyists and painters existed also, and singing at the services was usually obligatory. The larger monasteries were completely self-sufficient, and all the trades necessary for their maintenance seem to have been practised by the monks. Theodore of Studios favoured daily work and stressed the dignity of every task. But he also believed that life should be austere and fasts rigorously kept, and any infringement of the religious rules of the house was in the stricter establishments punished severely. Nor would the more pious priests and monastic authorities tolerate laxity on the part of secular officials or even the emperor himself. The interference of secular authorities in monastic affairs was deeply resented.

SCHISM BETWEEN EAST AND WEST

The incidents which led to the final schism between east and west in 1054 were no doubt political as well as religious, for the religious ones, centring round the inclusion of the phrase 'filioque' in the creed, hardly seem as we look back today to be fundamental. But it is very doubtful if the schism could have been averted even had political events not become tied up with arguments as to the essence of belief. The diversity of outlook between east and west was too profound to be healed. As Byzantine civilisation developed along its own very particular lines, the Church developed with it, and its thought gradually became more and more alienated from that of Rome. Just as Latin thought had, in classical times, been distinct from Greek, just as Byzantine art by the ninth century had become visibly different from Italian or Carolingian art, so the Byzantine religious outlook was distinct; east and west could hardly have been reconciled even had the will to blend been simultaneously present in both camps – which it was not. It had, in fact, been virtually inevitable that the two branches of the Christian faith should separate as early as the ninth century and any desire that there might have been for a *rapprochement* was, so far as the people were concerned, finally eliminated by the presence of westerners in the east as a result of the Crusades and the sack of Constantinople in 1204. The movement which had set out to free the holy cities from the infidel was actually the final straw that made any union of the Churches impossible, and which, as much as anything else, was responsible for the establishment of Islam over the whole of eastern Europe.

CHAPTER VII

Their Coins

THOUGH THE MAN who admires a certain degree of abstraction or formalism in art may well find that Byzantine mosaics and paintings exercise a greater appeal for him than does the realistic sculpture of Rome or the naturalistic painting of the Renaissance, it can hardly be argued that the coin engravers of the Byzantine empire ever achieved the same artistic heights as those who carved the coins of Greece or the medals of Italy. Yet the Byzantine coinage is by no means negligible either from the historical or the artistic point of view, for much of it is fine and all of it can throw considerable light on Byzantine civilisation as a whole. The designs are varied and often very attractive, the execution is in most cases at the very least competent, and a careful study brings out the fact that the portraits show more originality than they would seem to do at a first glance. Indeed, the coinage not only tells us a good deal about many of the individual emperors, but also reflects with remarkable clarity the changes and progress that took place throughout the course of Byzantine history.

Wroth, in his most excellent study of the coins in the British Museum, divides them into seven separate chronological groups. The earliest of these began with the reign of Arcadius (491) and extended to that of Constantine IV (685), for he argues that the coinage before about 490 was more Roman than Byzantine. Indeed, there was still a certain Roman character even in the coins of the sixth century. They bore on the obverse an imperial bust, in the square, solid style of those found on the Roman coins, and the inscriptions were in Latin or, as the period went on, in a sort of bilingual script, half Latin and half Greek. On the reverse there was at first a
Plate 59, *a*
figure, either the *Tyche* of a city, or a figure of St Michael,

derived from the classical winged victory; later a cross on a stepped pedestal became usual. But towards the end of the Plate 59, *e* period, as the Roman influence waned and the Greek elements became more predominant, the portraits tended to become at once more formal and at the same time more characterful – witness that of Phocas with pointed beard or that of the old Plate 59, *b* Heraclius, with long beard and immense moustache. Under Plate 59, *e* Justinian II the head of Christ appeared on the reverse, but in general an aniconic device like the cross was preferred; it is indeed not inappropriate that the coins of Heraclius, who was responsible for rescuing the True Cross from the Persians, should have borne this device; on some of them he even holds a cross himself. It is interesting to note that the love of symbolism which had characterised much Christian art before Constantine was so much to the fore on the coins; to many the suppression of any representation of the divine figure under the Iconoclasts cannot have seemed as anything untoward.

The most important factor regarding Wroth's second period, from Justinian II to Theodosius III (685–717), was a reduction in the number of mints, first because of Islamic conquests and thereafter as the result of imperial policy, according to which the conduct of affairs of state was concentrated more and more at Constantinople. The third period, from Leo III to Theophilus (717–842), coincides with the Iconoclast age, and was characterised not only by the omission of any religious figure on the coins, but also at times by the substitution for the cross of a second imperial portrait; to such Plate 59, *l* an extreme were the views on the dangers of religious art carried. The portraits of this age were conventional, angular and arid, and they contrast markedly with those of Wroth's fourth and fifth subdivisions, the one from Michael III to John I (842–976) and the other from Basil II to Constantine VIII (976–1081), when the whole coinage was distinguished by a vigour and a brilliance which clearly reflects the spirit of the great Macedonian dynasty. The reverse sides indicate the character of the times especially clearly. At first there was usually an inscription citing the imperial titles – apt pointer to the autocratic conception of the imperial dignity – and later the figure of Christ or the Virgin became usual, indicative of the conception of the emperor as Christ's vice-regent on earth and of the role of the Virgin as protectress of the capital city. Plate 59, *h, p, q* As time went on these figures tended to show greater elaboration. The emperors were thus shown enthroned or standing, while the head of Christ gave place to the figure of the Saviour enthroned, more than one variant in the rendering of the Virgin appeared, and sometimes even saints were depicted. This change corresponds closely with the growth in the power of the Church, just as the thin, poorer coins that became common in the period from Alexius I to Alexius IV (1081–1204) correspond with the period of economic difficulty and political decline characteristic of the Comnene age. The rather stiff portraits again are in keeping with the linear style that we see in the mosaics and paintings of the time, like the mosaic known as the John panel in Haghia Sophia (*c.* 1118).

The Latin emperors who ruled at Constantinople from 1204 till 1261 do not seem to have issued any coins; Venetian silver coins of rather Byzantine appearance were in general use at the time. But coins were struck at Salonica, Nicaea and Trebizond by the independent emperors ruling at those places. After 1261 minting was resumed at Constantinople Plate 59, *g* and the local mints were suppressed, except for that at Trebizond, which continued along with the independent empire there, till it was finally conquered by the Turks in 1461. Its coinage is interesting historically rather than very distinguished from the artistic point of view.

Plate 59, *r* The Palaeologue coins of Constantinople (1261–1453) are distinguished by minute and crowded designs and the subjects are often of a narrative character, such as the crowning of an emperor or a depiction of the city itself. Indeed, at no time does the art or the coinage of an age mirror so closely the nature of its history, for the latter had become one of minutiae, where campaign followed campaign, negotiation followed negotiation, and where a mass of minor individuals occupied the stage in rapid succession. The coins, like the individuals, lack monumentality of conception, even if the tale they tell is a vivid one.

Throughout the long history of the Byzantine coinage gold was the most important material. The principal unit was a coin weighing about sixty grains. It was first known as the *solidus*, then, in the Byzantine world, as the *nomisma* and finally, in the west, as the *bezant*. It enjoyed a world-wide circulation and was in fact the principal medium of exchange in international trade till the eleventh century, when confidence was to some extent lost owing to its debasement first by Michael IV (1034–1041) and then by Michael VII (1071–1078). The coinage was revalued by Alexius I (1081–1118), who issued *nomismata* of no less than seven different types. This may have helped the situation at home, but there was a general loss of confidence abroad, indicated by the fact that in a treaty Alexius made with Bohemond of Antioch it was stipulated that payment should be made in coins of his predecessor Michael and not in those issued during his own reign. In early times, that is until Constantine V (740–775), a half *solidus*, known as the *semissis*, and a third of a *solidus*, known as the *tremissis*, were also issued, and under Basil II there were two variants of the *nomisma*, a light and a heavy.

The gold coins were mostly minted at Constantinople; those in other metals were for a time also issued elsewhere. Thus silver coins are to be associated with Rome, Ravenna and Carthage; under Justinian I, bronze coins were struck at those places and in addition at Salonica, Nicomedia, Cyzicus, Antioch, Alexandria, Cherson and in Sicily. Under

Heraclius the same mints continued to operate, but their number declined from that time onwards. After the middle of the eighth century no Byzantine coins were made in Italy, and the north African and east Mediterranean mints ceased with the Islamic conquests. In Macedonian times all monetary operations were concentrated in Constantinople.

Silver coins are very rare today, and they were probably never as numerous as the gold coins. The principal one in early times was the *miliaresion*, but it varied in weight and type Plate 59, *f* from time to time. Heraclius instituted the issue of a new silver coin called the *hexagram*, but Constantine V substituted for this another type, distinguished by an inscription on the reverse. Alexius I coined a silver *nomisma*, and under An- Plate 59, *g* dronicus II yet another silver coin was issued, based on the Plate 59, *i* Venetian *grosso*. John V (1341–1391) issued a large silver coin known as the *hyperper*.

A distinctive system of bronze coinage was begun by Plate 59, *o* Anastasius I (491–518) who introduced the large bronze *follis* of forty *nummia*, marked on the reverse with a large M for forty. There were also coins of twenty, ten and five *nummia*, marked respectively K, I and E, and at Salonica and Alexandria coins of other values were also minted, like the Alexandrian twelve-*nummia* coin marked IB. These marks of value continued in use on the bronze coins till the Macedonian period, but they were completely discontinued after the time of Basil I, when divine figures, like those on the gold coins, were substituted.

In early times coins were occasionally dated to the year of a particular reign; the last instance of such a dating was on an issue of bronze coins in the thirtieth year of the reign of Constantine V (771). But there are a few other coins which can be dated more narrowly than to the reign as, for example, when Plate 59, *d* two imperial portraits appear, to mark the crowning of a joint emperor. An interesting instance of such exact dating is to be seen on certain coins of Theophilus; on the earlier issues he is shown alone but on the later ones with his empress Theodora and their three daughters; this can only have taken place after the death in 829 of his father Michael II, with whom he reigned till then as co-emperor.

A new type of coin, thin and concave in shape, known as *scyphati*, was introduced under Basil II and Constantine VIII (976–1025). They remained common thereafter, though they did not completely supplant the thicker coins of conventional form, for both types continued in use. One wonders why they were made, unless it was to show that their value was less, or to indicate that they were intended for use in a particular area, for example within the confines of the empire. Often their designs were rather finer than those on the thicker coins, and though it is hard to class them as other than decadent they are, none the less, attractive. As on the thick coins, the reverses are characterised by an increasing use of religious figures, Christ, the Virgin or even saints. St George thus appears on coins of John II (1118–1143) and St Theodore and St Demetrius on those of Manuel I (1143–1180), as well as the youthful head of the Saviour, Christ Emmanuel.

Until the time of Andronicus II (1282–1328) Byzantine coins seem to have been plentiful. After that, to judge by what has come down to us, they were fewer in number, and for a time there appears to have been no gold coinage at all, though it was restored by Manuel II (1391–1425). Had fate been less cruel and the course of events less inevitable, Manuel II would have been one of the really great Byzantine emperors. It is a fitting tribute to the character of this outstanding man that he was able to accomplish this last act, symbolising at the same time the imperial grandeur that had been and the economic rectitude that had made the *bezant* one of the most famous coins of history.

CHAPTER VIII

Their Art

Once out of nature I shall never take
My bodily form from any natural thing,
But such a form as Grecian goldsmiths make
Of hammered gold and gold enamelling
To keep a drowsy emperor awake;
Or set upon a golden bough to sing
To lords and ladies of Byzantium
Of what is past, or passing, or to come.

W. B. YEATS

SECULAR ART

TAKEN AS A WHOLE Byzantine art was a religious art and
a Christian art. There were of course exceptions, and
many things have come down to us that are of a purely secular
character, such as a number of mosaic pavements, the group
Plates 61–63 of ivories known as the Consular diptychs, and a large number of silver plates and dishes, all dating from before the eighth
Plate 69 century, and, in the middle period, some ivory caskets with
Plates 65–67 decorations culled from classical mythology, and some silks
and sculptures adorned with motifs of an oriental character.
And there was, of course, a good deal of jewellery intended for
personal use. But no large-scale secular decorations have survived, except for one room adorned with mosaics of the
Plate 71 twelfth century at Palermo, though the records tell of a chamber in the Great Palace at Constantinople called the Persian
House, which must have been rather similar to the room at
Palermo. Another hall in the Great Palace was adorned with
mosaics depicting the campaigns of Belisarius, while in
another there was an astonishing golden throne which could
be raised into the air, and there was a golden tree beside it,

with birds on it which twittered, and in front of it guardian lions that roared. It was made for the emperor Theophilus (829–842) and was the wonder of all who saw it. Several travellers have left descriptions of it. But like so much else from Byzantium, throne, mosaics and all the rest have perished, and we have only the descriptions telling of these wonders.

Our picture of Byzantine art is thus to a great extent one sided. But, as our examination of the history of Byzantium and of the lives and thought of the people has shown, religion played a more active part in life and thought than in most other states of mediaeval times, and it was almost certainly in the religious sphere that the most original and inspired productions of the Byzantine artists were to be found. The loss of the secular works has therefore not necessarily meant the loss of the best. Nor was the blend of east and west that made the religious art so distinctive ever really complete in the secular sphere.

HELLENISTIC ELEMENTS

A great deal of the secular art is strikingly Hellenistic. Thus the silver vessels, even those of as late as the seventh century, bear decorations of an entirely classical character, on the strength of which one would be tempted to assign the vessels to a pre-Christian date, did they not bear control stamps or 'hall-marks' which there is reason to believe were put on only in the Byzantine capital and which, for technical reasons, must in most cases have been added after the decorations had been completed. So classical are the designs that Matszulevitsch, who first published the important collection of silver vessels in the Hermitage Museum, coined the term 'The Byzantine Antique' to describe the style of their decoration. A somewhat similar style is also to be found in sculpture, even when the motifs are Christian. It is then usually termed the 'Neo-Attic'. Plate 53

The early ivories have less that is Greek about them, and it is not always easy to tell the Roman from the Byzantine examples. The great multiple imperial diptychs, like that of

Plate 60 Anastasius in the Louvre known as the Barberini ivory, or that of which the ivory of Ariadne at Florence formed a part, are undoubtedly Constantinopolitan and have all the dignity and magnificence one associates with the Byzantine court. The former is especially interesting because of the tribute bearers shown at the bottom, conquered barbarians from the north on one side and an embassy from India on the other. The ivories issued by the Consuls when they came to office are on the other hand not always so obviously Constantinopolitan, and did we not know the names of the Consuls, one of whom was appointed to Rome and one to Constantinople each year, it would not always be easy to distinguish the western from the eastern ivories. Rather, the differences between them seem to indicate something of the character of the men for whom they
Plate 61 were made. Thus the decoration of that of Flavius Anastasius in the Cabinet des Médailles (517) is grandiose and rather
Plate 62 pompous. That of Magnus (518) is dignified, yet devoid of
Plate 63 ostentation, while that of Justinian, now at Milan (521), shows a restraint which would satisfy even the most exacting of the critics of today when exuberance is eschewed.

THE EASTERN LEGACY

If the ivories and the silver attest links with classical art, the legacy of the east is equally clear in other arts, notably the
Plate 41 jewellery and the textiles. Theodora, in the lovely mosaic in San Vitale at Ravenna, thus wears a crown derived from a Sasanian prototype, while the profusion of jewels that adorn her person attests an oriental taste, and her costume is Persian rather than Roman. The rich textiles of which the robes of her courtiers must have been made are again of oriental inspiration.
Plates 65–67 Indeed, the designs of textiles from that time onwards tended to become more and more eastern. Such motifs as the lion-headed bird, or that of two birds or animals confronted with a stylised vase or tree between them, were taken over directly from Persia, and other motifs, like that of the archer, were disposed in a similar oriental way. After the ninth century the

kufic script was also often used for decorative purposes. In view of the very oriental character of the motifs, it is often hard to determine where many of the famous silks were woven. Some of them bear inscriptions in Greek citing the names of emperors or stating that they were made in the imperial workshops at Constantinople, but more often such inscriptions are absent, and there is nothing in the designs and little in the technique to distinguish the products of one centre from those of another. A good deal of work that was closely similar to the Constantinopolitan was certainly done in Syria both before and after the Islamic conquest; Greece was important by the eleventh century, if not before, and in the twelfth the workshops of Sicily were modelled on those of the Byzantine world and Byzantine craftsmen were employed in them.

QUALITY OF DESIGN

Most of this secular art is of very high quality, and a study of it can help to an understanding of the social life and the tastes of the Byzantine upper classes. Thus the ivories are all outstanding, whatever their style. The silver plates all show a fine sense of design, and the relief is low, so that even the most ornate of the dishes are eminently practical; there is none of that absence of good taste which made so much Roman silver so totally unusable and at the same time so monstrously hideous. From this one might deduce not only that there was a marked delicacy of taste, but also that the Byzantines showed a practical sense and were not carried away by the vulgarities of ostentation. The decorations also serve to bear out the attention paid to classical learning and the closeness of trading links with the east.

In the art of the great middle period, from the ninth to the twelfth centuries, the blend in the religious sphere was even more complete, while the patronage was if anything even more exacting. However, it becomes rather easier to distinguish the products of the capital from those of provincial centres or from things made in the west in imitation of Byzantine models. An

Plate 69 ivory like the exquisite Veroli casket in the Victoria and Albert
Museum is thus obviously to be assigned to the capital, while
Plate 68 one like that in the Palazzo Venezia at Rome was probably
made elsewhere; Strzygowski has even suggested that Armenian
craftsmen were responsible. A rather unusual casket at Sens,
with twelve sides, is no doubt a western work in the Byzantine
manner. Examples like these serve to attest the admiration that
existed elsewhere for the best Byzantine works, as well as to
show the freedom with which ideas travelled at this time;
Germany, France, Italy, even Britain, were alike affected, and
work was done in all these places in imitation of Byzantine
prototypes. Another secular casket which is especially significant
Plate 70 in this connection is preserved at Troyes; on the top are
mounted figures, presumably imperial, on the sides hunting
scenes, suggestive of some of the early floor mosaics, and at the
ends birds wholly Chinese in character. The casket is Byzantine,
but the ends must have been inspired by a drawing or a
textile imported from the Far East, just as the caskets, textiles
and reliquaries made in the west were inspired by Byzantine
models. It is probably the first instance of Chinoiserie in the
history of art.

The copying of Byzantine models elsewhere must have begun at a very early date. Of course Christian art as a whole, both in the Byzantine world and in the west, owed a considerable debt to what had been done previously, so that when objects which we know to be western resemble those we know to be Byzantine, the possibility that the similarities are due to a common ancestry must always be borne in mind. This applies, for example, to much Carolingian art, which was inspired by early Christian works done in Rome or elsewhere in Italy. But others owe an undoubted debt to Byzantium, as is the case, for example, with Charlemagne's mortuary chapel at Aachen[1] or

[1] Aachen was probably modelled on San Vitale at Ravenna. Some authorities, notably Ward Perkins, 'The Italian Element in Late Roman and Early

the paintings in the church of Müstair in Switzerland, while miniatures of the Ada group would often seem to owe a debt to Byzantium also. These instances of direct Byzantine influence are more numerous in Ottonian than in Carolingian art, partly because Early Christian prototypes had by then become less numerous, and partly because contacts with Byzantium had been intensified as a result of intermarriages and diplomatic and trade exchanges. And the Ottonian age coincided with that in which Byzantine religious art was in its most active and characteristic phase.

RELIGIOUS ART

The religious art of the great middle period of Byzantium was marked by a complete fusion of the various elements that had played a part in its formation, Greek and Roman on the one hand and Persian and Semetic on the other. There has, however, been a good deal of argument as to when the fusion was actually accomplished. It had gone quite far, though it was a long way from being universal, by the end of the fifth century. But that age was still in the main primarily 'Early Christian'. As our examination of the architecture has shown, the new style was fully mature by Justinian's day, and the decoration of the various churches he built bears this out. The capitals and cornices are thus in a wholly new manner, where low relief and an almost abstract design replace the high relief and naturalism of classical times, while the mosaic decoration is of a rather more symbolic character and blends in a new way into the spatial conception of the building. In fact, in Justinian's Haghia Sophia we see a wholly new art, at once far

---

Mediaeval Architecture', *Proceedings of the British Academy*, XXXIII, 1947, maintain that San Vitale could have been worked out on the basis of what existed previously in Italy, and is to be regarded as an Italian and not a Byzantine building. Others, notably C. Delvoye, 'Sur la date de la Fondation de Saints Sergius et Bacchus à Constantinople et de San Vitale à Ravènne', *Coll. Latomos*, XLIV, Bruxelles, 1960, p. 263, hold that SS. Sergius and Bacchus was earlier in date and that San Vitale was modelled upon it.

better suited to Christian needs than a purely classical style and also far more impressive than anything that the east had produced or was likely to produce. Haghia Sophia represents something fresh in art, and the profound emotion that it engenders is there even today in a building where much of the decoration and furnishings that formed a part of it has perished and which has now been secularised and divorced from all its original associations.

As stated above, Haghia Sophia was not Justinian's only great foundation, and there were numerous decorations in the new style; the mosaics of San Vitale, St Apollinare Nuovo and St Apollinare in Classe at Ravenna are the most important that survive. They are in a provincial centre, but it is hard to believe that any mosaic could be more beautiful than that of the procession of male and female saints on the side walls of St Apollinare Nuovo, which was set up about 561. Surely we see here work comparable with the very best that was being done in the capital itself?

So far as we can tell from the rather scanty monuments that survive, there were no great changes in art during the next two centuries, and with Iconoclasm religious art was banned, though if we may judge from the mosaics at Damascus, done, the records tell us, by Byzantine craftsmen for an Islamic patron in 715, a decoration which was both beautiful and inspiring could also be wholly aniconic. But with the lifting of the ban in 843 a mass of great works seems at once to have been set in hand. Among the earliest of them were the mosaics in the sanctuary of the church of the Assumption at Nicaea, destroyed in 1922. Those in Haghia Sophia at Salonica were probably done between 842 and 850, and the archangel in front of the apse of Haghia Sophia at Constantinople must date from around the middle of the century. On a smaller scale the miniatures of the Paris Psalter (Paris Gr. 139) in the Bibliothèque Nationale are again to be assigned to the period im-

Plates 72, 73

Plate 74

mediately succeeding Iconoclasm, while the more numerous ones in the lovely Homilies of Gregory Nazianzus (Paris, Gr. 510) in the same library were painted under the patronage of Basil I (867–886). All these are works of art of outstanding quality, and it seems inconceivable that such fine things could have been produced unless technical training had continued throughout Iconoclast times. As it was, the years that followed the end of Iconoclasm were some of the most fruitful in the whole history of Byzantine art.

Plate 57

MOSAICS

The art of the Second Golden Age saw its fullest development in mosaics. These depended in the main on court patronage, for in any case until the eleventh century only the court was powerful and rich enough to sponsor large-scale decorations, and it was only in these that the ideas and ideals of the new art could be fully realised. Numerous churches in the capital were decorated at this time on the model of Basil I's Nea. None of these survives, but mosaics at Hosios Lukas, Chios and Daphni in Greece serve to indicate the quality and character of what was done. The loveliness of the colouring can really only be appreciated on the spot, but the transcendental conception is obvious from reproductions. The mosaics of Daphni afford an admirable illustration. In the scene of the Annunciation, for example, which occupies one of the squinches below the dome, the space between the angel and the Virgin is in some ways the most significant part of the picture – more significant even than the figures themselves. Indeed, the scenes constituted an essential accompaniment to each section of the church's architecture; the dome, the conch, the pendentives or the arches, each took on the role of a setting for the picture there situated, and the church as a whole became the background for the composite series. It was as incomplete without its mosaics as the façade of a Gothic cathedral would be incomplete without its sculptures. Church and decoration thus formed a unity, spiritual in character, sacred in essence. The

Plate 75

system passed, along with other elements of Byzantine sculpture, to Russia, but it was essentially foreign to the western world.

RELIGIOUS BASIS OF MINOR ARTS

A similar preoccupation with religious themes characterised the minor arts, more especially the ivories and the works in metal and enamel. The ivories are especially outstanding, and

Plate 78

the lovely Harbaville triptych in the Louvre or a rather similar

Plate 77

one in the British Museum bearing the Crucifixion are typical in the profound spirituality of their conception, while the theme of divine sanction dominates even in the imperial portraits, like

Plate 38

that of the crowning of Romanus and Eudoxia. Nearly all the examples of metalwork and enamel that we know also have a religious connotation, in that they form parts of reliquaries,

Plates 78–81

gospel covers, chalices and so forth. Practically the only excep-

Plate 76

tions are crowns, like that of Constantine Monomachos at Budapest. Precious materials like rock crystal or onyx were extensively used for the religious vessels, and glass was probably similarly employed, though little has survived. So far as we can tell it was only metal and pottery that were normally employed for everyday use. A large number of different techniques

Figs. 29, 30

of pottery making can be distinguished, and the forms were often quite eleborate. Even if Byzantine pottery is only seldom quite as beautiful as Islamic, it is often, none the less, of real quality. Nearly all the examples we have come from excavations, and a study of them is likely to prove of increasing importance for mediaeval archaeology as a whole. Already it has served to substantiate the importance of trade relations with places as far away as Britain.

Though the art of the great middle period of Byzantine history is of a very distinctive type, it was by no means uniform in style. Thus as the eleventh century passed into the twelfth a more linear manner came into vogue, as a comparison of the

Plates 82, 83

two sets of imperial portraits in Haghia Sophia, the Zoe panel done about 1042 and the John panel, dated to 1118, serves to

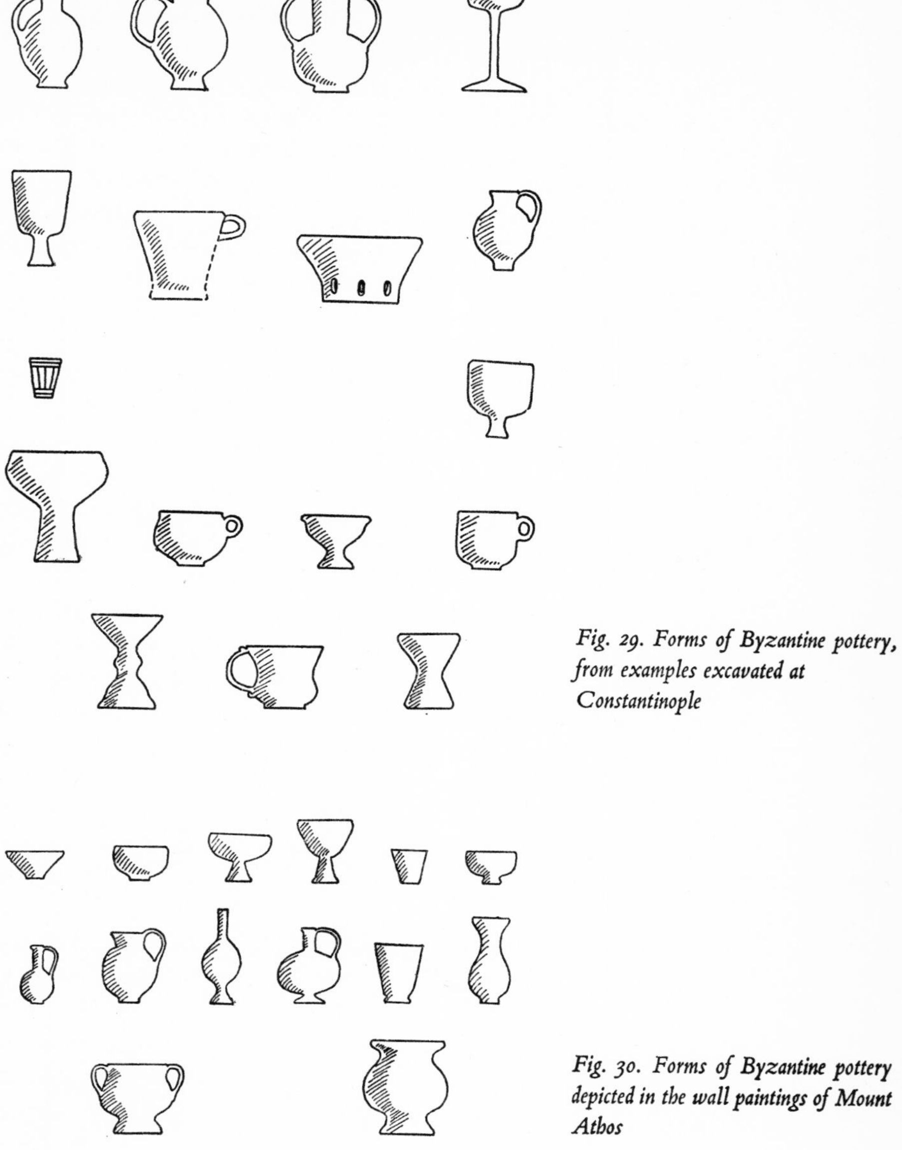

Fig. 29. Forms of Byzantine pottery, from examples excavated at Constantinople

Fig. 30. Forms of Byzantine pottery depicted in the wall paintings of Mount Athos

indicate, while in the countryside church decorations became more concerned with narrative and less with esoteric theology. There, and in the poorer churches of the city, full-length portraits of saints took the place of the marble revetments that adorned the lower levels of the walls of the richer churches, while up above the number of the scenes was multiplied. They also came to be drawn from more diverse sources, the lives of the saints to whom a particular church or chapel was dedicated often being depicted in addition to the more conventional scenes from the lives of Christ or the Virgin. And in the depiction of these scenes a livelier, more intimate manner came into vogue and a new interest in humanism was developed.

THE BYZANTINE RENAISSANCE

This new twelfth-century style is exemplified in concrete form in the pose of the Virgin in the icon known as Our Lady of
Plate 84 Vladimir, now in the Tretiakov gallery at Moscow, which
must have been painted in Constantinople about 1125. The
Plate 86 old hieratic pose of the Hodegetria, where the Mother points
Plate 85 to the Child, or the still more impersonal one of the Nikopea
type, where the Child appears on a medallion, have given place to a greater intimacy, for the Child's face is pressed against the Virgin's in affection. Milković-Pepek has called attention to the fact that a similar intimate approach is to be seen in wall paintings at Ochrid in Macedonia, even as early as the eleventh century, and we must conclude that the new humanistic out-
Plate 83 look was developing alongside the linear manner of the John
panel, which has hitherto been regarded as typical of the Comnene age. Indeed, recent research suggests that there were two very distinct styles in vogue in the twelfth century, the one severe and linear, the other showing greater humanism and expression; it is perhaps best respresented by the wall paintings
Plate 87 at Nerez, dated from 1164.

But the new style was only fully developed in the thirteenth century, and owing to the Latin occupation of Constantinople, which lasted from 1204 till 1261; the first large-scale monuments

Plate 88

Plate 89

are to be found outside the capital, in Russia, in Bulgaria, at Trebizond, and more particularly in Yugoslavia. Most important of them are the wall paintings at Mileševa (1235) and Sopoćani (*c.* 1260). In both places the work is of very high quality and shows a fully developed humanistic approach. In the capital itself the first large-scale decoration in the new manner is a mosaic in Haghia Sophia representing the Deesis. Its date has been disputed. Whittemore, who uncovered it, would assign it to the early twelfth century, or even to the eleventh. Demus has suggested a date around 1265, so much does it resemble monuments of the Palaeologue period. Lazarev favours the middle of the twelfth century, seeing similarities to mosaics at Cefalu. The grandeur of the composition would seem to support Lazarev's dating, for it is hard to equate so monumental a work with the opening years of the Palaeologue empire.

KARIYE CAMII

Plate 91

There is, on the other hand, no disputing the date of the most important and glorious examples of the Palaeologue style, the mosaics and paintings of the little church of the Chora in Constantinople, usually known by its Turkish name of Kariye Camii. The work there dates from between about 1305 and 1315. The mosaics comprise numerous single figures and a whole series of scenes from the lives of Christ and the Virgin. The wall paintings, which are in a side chapel or *pareccleseion*, are mostly concerned with the after life, for the chapel was a mortuary one. Outstanding among them is the scene of Christ's Descent into Limbo, which, in Byzantine art, was the normal way of depicting the Resurrection. All the scenes, whether in paint or mosaic, are full of expression and lively detail, and the whole decoration is a thing of surprising beauty and enchantment. But though they show great vividness, there is nothing at Kariye that is not truly Byzantine. It is quite unnecessary to suggest the participation of Italian craftsmen or the use of Italian models, as authorities at one time tended to do. We see here, and in numerous other decorations of the age at Constantinople, Salonica, Mistra and elsewhere, the last flowering of the long-lived Byzantine style. It was a fresh, delicate and very delightful flower, and deserves just as much consideration as the more impressive blooms of earlier centuries.

This new style in mosaic and painting was paralleled by a revival in literature, and some secular writing of considerable interest was produced. The evidence furnished by this and the art suggests that though faith was by no means dead, the old passion for theological argument and the old transcendental outlook had both to some extent been superseded. The economic and political situation had also changed, and by the fourteenth century the great nobles were playing a more important role as patrons than were the emperors. The decoration of Kariye
Plate 95 Camii was thus sponsored by a certain Theodore Metochites and there are fine manuscripts which were done for such men as
Plate 94 the High Admiral Apocaucos or John Cantacuzenos; though the latter became an emperor he, like Apocaucos, was originally a member of the powerful aristocracy. The rich silks in which they are clothed in their portraits serve to show that the Byzantine weavers had lost none of their skill, and there are other treasures of this last age which are no less sumptuous, even if they were fewer than in the great tenth century. The state may have been impoverished and weak; the high standards of quality remained.

THE BYZANTINE LEGACY

So far as Byzantine history is concerned, the story ends with the conquest of Constantinople in 1453. But this did not mean that the production of works of art ceased. Indeed, a very great deal was achieved in the way of painting, especially panel painting, after that date. The styles that had been evolved from the Byzantine basis in Slav lands had by then already become national, and after the fifteenth century we can hardly speak of these areas as Byzantine in more than a very general sense. Greece was the direct heir, the Slav lands—Russia in particular—were the more influential ones and the wall paintings, icons and embroideries produced in those lands were often of very great quality; they serve to show that Byzantine art did not die with the fall of the empire, but survived down to quite recent times along with the Orthodox faith with which it had from the outset been so closely linked. It thus constituted the longest lived style of western art. But it was not so much its duration as its intrinsic quality that distinguished it, and of all the arts of the Christian era none was a truer or more loyal servant of the faith to which it was dedicated or a more profound mirror of the age that produced it.

Bibliography

Though very little has been written on the people themselves or on the geography of the Byzantine world, books on other aspects of Byzantine civilisation are numerous in all the major European languages. It would be quite outside the scope of this work to attempt to give a full bibliography. The list given here is confined to the more important general and in the main fairly recent books; in all of them fuller bibliographies relating to the branches of the study with which they deal will be found.

History

HUSSEY, J. M. *The Byzantine World.* London. 1957.

OSTROGORSKY, G. *History of the Byzantine State.* Oxford. 1956. Also in French and German.

VASILIEV, A. A. *History of the Byzantine Empire.* Madison. 1928. Also in French.

Civilisation

BAYNES, N. H. *Byzantine Studies and other Essays.* London. 1955.

BAYNES, N. H., and MOSS, H. ST L. B. *Byzantium. An Introduction to East Roman Civilisation.* Oxford. 1948.

BRÉHIER, L. *Vie et Mort de Byzance.* Paris. 1948

HAUSSIG, H. W. *Kulturgeschichte von Byzanz.* Stuttgart. 1959.

HOUSTON, M. G. *Ancient Greek, Roman and Byzantine Costume.* London. 1947.

RUNCIMAN, S. *Byzantine Civilisation.* London. 1933.

Religion

BECK, H. C. *Kirche und theologische Literatur im byzantinischen Reich.* Munich. 1959.

ZERNOV, N. *Eastern Christendom.* London. 1961.

Architecture

EBERSOLT, J. *Monuments d'Architecture byzantine.* Paris. 1934.

HAMILTON, J. A. *Byzantine Architecture and Decoration.* London. 1933. Revised 1956.

STEWART, C. Revised edition of *Simpson's History of Architectural Development, vol. II. Early Christian, Byzantine and Romanesque.* London. 1954.

Coins

WROTH, W. *Catalogue of the Imperial Byzantine Coins in the British Museum.* London. 1908.

Art

GRABAR, A. *Byzantine Painting.* London. 1953. Also in French and German.

TALBOT RICE, D. *The Art of Byzantium.* London. 1959. Also in German, French and Italian.

TALBOT RICE, D. *Byzantine Art.* Harmondsworth. Revised edition 1961. Also in Italian.

LAZAREV, V. *History of Byzantine Painting.* Moscow. 1947. In Russian.

3

4

5

6

7

8

9

12

13

14

15

16

17

20

21

24

25

26

2

32

35

33

36

34

37

40

39

41

42

43

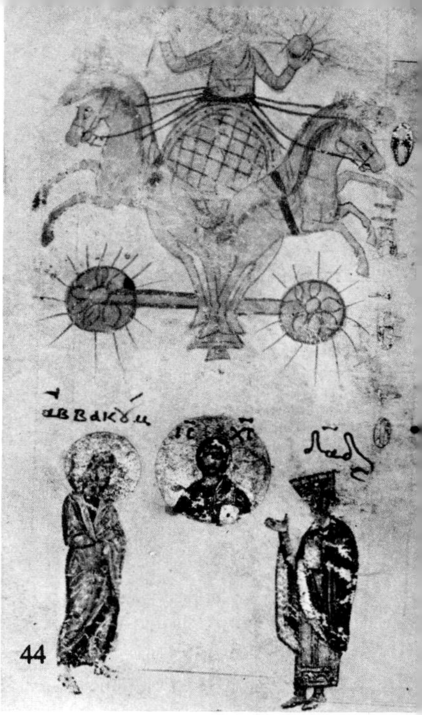

44

46

47

48

50

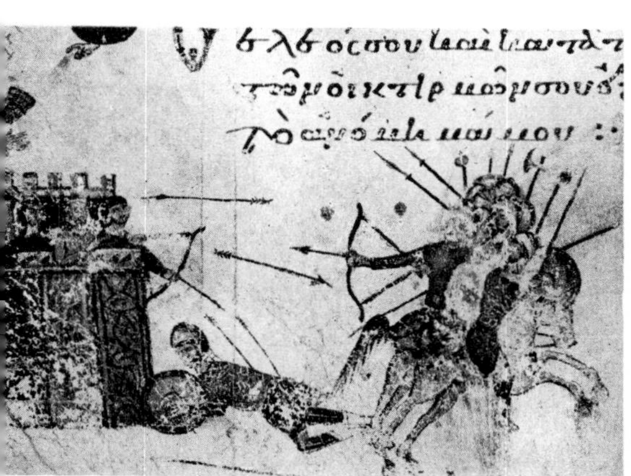

52

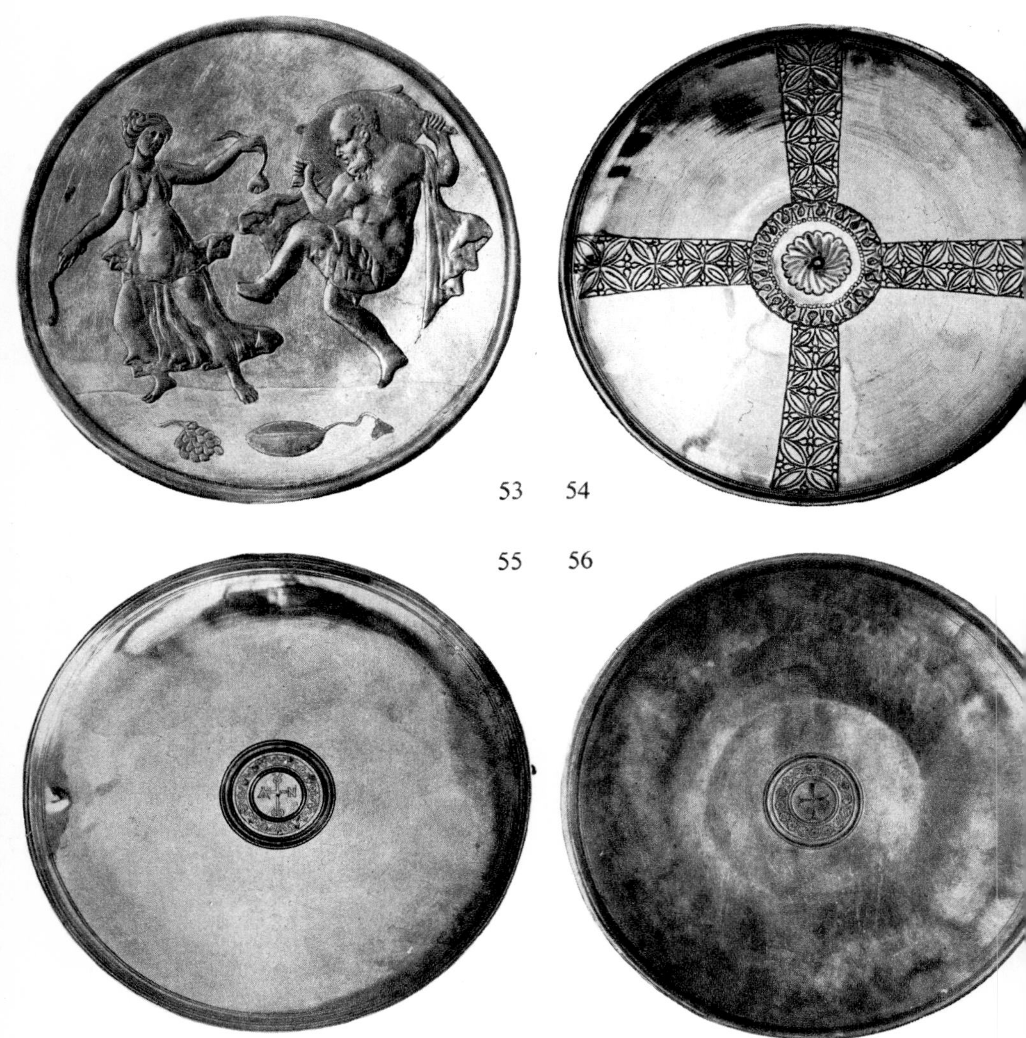

53 54

55 56

ϹΥΝΟΔΟϹΔΕΥΤΕΡΑ

ΜΕΓΑϹ
Ο ΘϹ ΤΩΝ
ΧΡΙϹΤΙ
ΑΝΩΝ:

a
b
c
d
e
f
g
h
i
j
k
l
m
n
o
p
q
r

FL·ANASTASIVS·PAVLVS·PROBVS·
SABINIAN·POMPEIVS·ANASTASIVS·

62

FL·PETR·SABBAT·IVSTINIAN·V·I·
MVNERA PAR
VA QVIDEM PRE
TIO SED HONO
RIBVS ALMA

63

4

65

66

67

ΘΗCΑΥΡ CΑΦΡΩΝΨΥΗ ΛΩΝ ΠΑΝΤΟΚΡΑΤΟΡ ΗCΗΨΥΧΗΚCΚ

70 *a*

70 *b*

70 *c*

2

73

5

77

78

79

80

81

82

83

84

85

86

87

88

89

90

91

92

93

Notes on the Plates

1 Constantinople. Part of the land walls. Fifth century. *Photo Hirmer.*

2 Constantinople. Part of the sea walls. Fifth century. *Photo Sender.*

3 Constantinople. Aqueduct, probably built under Andronicus I Comnenus (1183–1185). Repaired under Sultan Suleiman I. *Photo Talbot Rice.*

4 Constantinople. The Golden Gate. Fifth century. *Photo Talbot Rice.*

5 Constantinople. Cistern close to the church of St Eirene. Sixth century. *Photo Talbot Rice.*

6 Constantinople. Underground water conduit. Probably sixth century. *Photo Talbot Rice.*

7 Constantinople. The Yeri-batan-Serai cistern (underground palace). Sixth century. *Photo Hirmer.*

8 Constantinople. Remains of the triumphal arch of Theodosius I. *c.* 390. *Photo Talbot Rice.*

9 Constantinople. Base of the obelisk of Theodosius I. *c.* 390. *Photo Talbot Rice.*

10 Constantinople. Substructure of the Great Palace, showing brick vaulting systems. Sixth century. *Photo Walker Trust.*

11 Constantinople. Substructure of 'The House of Justinian', showing concrete construction. *Photo Walker Trust.*

12 Constantinople. Substructure of the Great Palace, showing types of masonry construction. *Photo Walker Trust.*

13 Constantinople. Church of SS. Sergius and Bacchus. 526–537. *Photo Powell.*

14 Constantinople. Church of Haghia Sophia. Capital. 532–537. *Photo Talbot Rice.*

15 Constantinople. Church of Haghia Sophia. Capital. 532–537. *Photo Talbot Rice.*

16 Constantinople. Church of St Eirene. Interior. 532. *Photo Powell.*

17 Constantinople. Substructure of the Great Palace, showing stonework. Probably fifth century. *Photo Walker Trust.*

18 Constantinople. Haghia Sophia. Exterior from south. 532–537. *Photo Powell.*

19 Constantinople. Haghia Sophia. Interior. 532–537. *After Fossati.*

20 Daphni, near Athens. Church. *c.* 1100. *Photo Talbot Rice.*

21 Nerez, Yugoslavia. Church. *c.* 1164. *Photo Talbot Rice.*

22 Constantinople. Church of Kariye Camii. Eleventh century and later. *Photo Talbot Rice.*

23 Hosios Lukas, Greece. The northern church. Eleventh century. *Photo Talbot Rice.*

24 Salonica. Church of the Holy Apostles. *c.* 1312. To show ornamental brickwork at the east end. *Photo Talbot Rice.*

25 Constantinople. 'The House of Justinian'. Eighth century. *Photo Walker Trust.*

26 Ravenna. St Apollinare Nuovo. Mosaic: the Palace. Sixth century. *Photo Alinari.*

27 Constantinople. The so-called 'Palace of Constantine Porphyrogenitus'. Fourteenth century. *Photo Hirmer.*

28 Mount Athos. The Monastery of Chilandari. *Photo Robert Byron.*

29 Mount Athos. The Monastery of St Paul. *Photo Robert Byron.*

30 Ochrid, Yugoslavia. St Sophia. The west front. *c.* 1317. *Photo De Roko.*

31 Mount Athos. The Monastery of Simopetra. *Photo Robert Byron.*

32, 33 Constantinople. Mosaic floor of the Great Palace. Peasants cultivating and caring for their flocks. Sixth century. *Photos Walker Trust.*

34 Miniature from a copy of the Gospels of the eleventh century. Bibliothèque Nationale, Paris. Gr. 74, f. 39 v. Payment of workers and work in the vineyards. *Library photo.*

35, 36 Miniatures from a psalter in the British Museum, Add. 19352. Dated 1066. f. 170. Masons at work. f. 36. Peasants digging. *Museum photos.*

37 Miniatures from a copy of the Homilies of Gregory Nazianzus of the eleventh century. Bibliothèque Nationale, Gr. 533, f. 34. Scenes of peasant life. *Library photo.*

38 Ivory: the crowning of Romanus and Eudoxia by Christ. Tenth century. The Cabinet des Médailles, Paris. Height 24·5 cm. *Photo Hirmer.*

39 Ivory: the Empress Ariadne. *c.* 500. Museo Nazionale, Florence. Height 36·5 cm. *Photo Hirmer.*

40 Miniature: the Emperor Basil II, conqueror of the Bulgars. 976–1025. The Marcian Library, Venice, Cod. Gr. 17. Height of MS. 39·5 cm. *Photo Hirmer.*

41 Ravenna. San Vitale. Mosaic. The Empress Theodora and her court. 526–547. *Photo Alinari.*

42 Ravenna. St Apollinare Nuovo. Mosaic. Procession of female saints on the north wall. *c.* 561. *Photo Alinari.*

43 Constantinople. Mosaic from the Great Palace. Gladiators in the Hippodrome wearing the *segmenta* of the Green faction. Sixth century. *Photo Walker Trust.*

44 Miniature from a psalter in the British Museum, Add. 19352. Dated 1066. f. 61 v. A four-horse chariot. *Museum photo.*

45 Textile. A four-horse chariot. Musée du Cinquentenaire, Brussels. Eighth century. Height 25 cm. Width 78 cm. *Photo Byzantine Exhibition, 1958 (No. 49).*

46, 47, 48 Constantinople. Mosaics from the Great Palace. Sixth century. Hare hunt. Man kicked from mule. Spearman. *Photos Walker Trust.*

49 Lesnovo, Yugoslavia. Wall painting illustrating Psalm 150. 1341–1349. *Photo Yugoslav Conservation Department.*

50 Miniature from an Octateuch, Vatican. Gr. 747. Eleventh century. Weaver. The miniature illustrates the text of Exodus XXXVI, where the task of preparing hangings to decorate a sanctuary is described. *Photo Courtauld Institute.*

51, 52 Miniatures from a psalter in the British Museum, Add. 19352. Dated 1066. f. 63 v. Attack on a fortress. f. 201. A Boat. *Museum photos.*

53 Silver dish from near Perm, Russia. Now in the State Hermitage Museum, Leningrad. A Satyr and a Maenad. Dated 610–629. Diameter 25·7 cm. *Photo Hirmer.*

54 Dish of Byzantine workmanship from Sutton Hoo. Now in the British Museum. Diameter 22·7 cm. *Museum photo.*

55 Dish from near Kyrenia, Cyprus. Now in the Nicosia Museum. At the centre a cruciform monogram. Dated 602–610. Diameter 44 cm. *Photo Byzantine Exhibition, 1958 (No. 38).*

56 Dish from the district of Perm, Russia. In the State Hermitage Museum, Leningrad. Sixth century. Diameter 26 cm. The dish bears a control stamp of Constantinople. *Museum photo.*

57 Miniature from the Homilies of Gregory Nazianzus, done for the Emperor Basil I around 880. The picture represents the Second Oecumenical Council, held at Constantinople in 362, with the Gospels open on the throne to indicate Christ's presence. Bibliothèque Nationale, Paris. Gr. 510, f. 355. *Library photo.*

58 Miniature, showing the Emperor John Cantacuzenus, on the left as Emperor, and on the right as a monk, after his abdication, under the name of Joseph. From a manuscript in the Bibliothèque Nationale, Paris, Gr. 1242, f. 123 v. 1370–1375. *Library photo.*

59 Coins. Photograph and notes kindly supplied by Mr P. D. Whitting, G.M.

a. *Solidus* of Maurice (582–602); obverse and reverse. Obv. Bust of Maurice facing, wearing the cuirass of a Roman soldier and carrying a shield with a horseman device over his left shoulder. Rev. A winged St Michael, successor to the Winged Victory of Classical art, advancing with a staff bearing the Christogram in his right hand.

b. *Solidus* of Phocas (602–610); obverse only. Probably issued in 603, this coin shows Phocas in the consular shirt and *trabea*, with the *mappa* in his right hand. Note his characteristic pointed beard and contrast the portraits of Maurice (*a*) and Heraclius (*c*, *d* and *e*).

c. *Solidus* of Heraclius (610–641); obverse only. Issued between 610 and 613, the coin shows Heraclius as a young man wearing a cuirass with *paludamentum* over it.

d. *Solidus* of Heraclius (610–641); obverse only. Issued between 613 and 629. Heraclius associated his son with him as emperor at this time; both are shown wearing a *paludamentum*, which covers their other robes.

e. *Solidus* of Heraclius (610–641); obverse and reverse. Issued between 629 and 631, after the conclusion of the Persian wars which began in 613. Heraclius has moustaches and a long beard and his son a close beard. The reverse bears the 'cross on steps' design popular on many pre-Iconoclast coins; it is from the Ravenna mint, unlike the obverse, which is Constantinopolitan.

f. *Milaresion* of Heraclius (610–641); obverse only. Issued in 629. Heraclius is in military uniform and is crowned by Victory. He holds in his right hand the Holy Cross which he had recaptured from the Persians and returned to Jerusalem in 629.

g. *Grosso* of Andronicus II (1282–1328) and his son Michael IX; obverse only. Issued between 1295 and 1320. This coin was copied from the Venetian *grosso* and was intended as its Byzantine equivalent. Once the *solidus* had been debased the coinage of the Italian trading cities became the international currency.

h. *Milaresion* of Basil II (976–1025) and his brother Constantine VIII; obverse only. The legend repeats the motto of Constantine the Great, EN TOVTW NIKA, and the 'cross on steps' theme (see *e*) can be seen persisting. The three rings were intended to discourage clipping, but were not always successful, for perfect examples are rare.

i. *Hyperper* of John V (1341–1391); obverse only. These larger silver pieces took the place of the gold *solidus* or its larger but thinner form the *nomisma*, the steady weight and quality of which had made it the international currency of the day. Debasement of the gold used began in the eleventh century (see *k*).

j. *Follis* of Justinian I (527–565); obverse and reverse. Obv. from the mint of Nicomedia, dated 539/540. Rev. from the mint of Constantinople, dated 539. That year represents regnal year XII, the first year in which this coin was issued.

k. *Nomisma* of Constantine IX (1042–1055); obverse only. The *solidus* or *nomisma* was originally issued in gold of 23 to 24 carat. The standard of weight and purity was maintained until the reign of Michael IV (1034–1041). The piece illustrated is of 19½ carat.

l. *Solidus* of Nicephorus I (802–811); obverse and reverse. The Iconoclast emperors put other members of the family on the reverse instead of any Christian symbol. In this case it is the Emperor's son, Stauracius. The effect of Iconoclasm on portraiture may be seen if this coin is compared with *e*.

m. *Solidus* of Philippicus Bardanes (711–713); obverse only. This shows the elaborate *loros* developed from the consular scarf and associated with the religious functions of the emperor; also, and exceptionally at this date, the Emperor holds the consular sceptre with eagle head.

n. *Nomisma* of John II Comnenus (1118–1143); obverse only. This is typical of later Byzantine gold pieces in having standing figures instead of a bust. The portrait of John II, small as it is, may be compared with the mosaic depicting him in the south gallery of Haghia Sophia (Pl. 83).

o. *Follis* of Leo VI (886–912); obverse only. The Emperor holds the *labarum,* linking him with Constantine the Great, and is seated on a throne which should be compared with that shown in the mosaic of the same period over the western door of Haghia Sophia.

p. *Nomisma* of Alexius I (1081–1118); obverse and reverse. This coin represents an extreme example of the Byzantine liking for elongated figures and unusual perspective. Alexius I reorganised the coinage and endeavoured to restore the weight and purity of the *nomisma* to something like its original standard. On the reverse, Christ is shown enthroned, with His right hand raised in blessing.

q. *Nomisma* of Andronicus I (1183–1185); reverse only. The Virgin is shown seated, holding a medallion of the infant Christ before her.

r. *Nomisma* of Michael VIII (1261–1282); obverse and reverse. The imaginative designs of the Palaeologan period deserved better technical execution, more particularly with regard to the fine design on the reverse of this coin, showing the Virgin Orans in the midst of the walls and towers of Constantinople. The obverse represents the Archangel Michael supporting the Emperor on his knees before Christ enthroned on the right. After this reign a new series of debasements began until, at the end of the century, the *nomisma* became a silver coin (*see i*).

60 Ivory, known as the Barberini ivory. The Louvre Museum, Paris. The Emperor is probably to be identified as Anastasius. and the ivory to be dated to about 500. Height 34·1 cm. Width 26·6 cm. *Photo Hirmer.*

61 Ivory. Right leaf of the diptych of Flavius Anastasius. 517. Cabinet des Médailles, Bibliothèque Nationale, Paris. Height 36 cm. Width 13 cm. The consul is seated, holding *mappa* and sceptre; below are circus scenes. *Photo Hirmer.*

62 Ivory. Leaf of the diptych of Magnus. 518. Cabinet des Médailles, Bibliothèque Nationale, Paris. Height 26·2 cm. Width 13 cm. The leaf has at some time been cut; there was probably an inscription above and a scene below. *Photo Hirmer.*

63 Ivory. Leaf of the diptych of Justinianus. 521. The Castello Sforzesco, Milan. Height 36·8 cm. Width 12·7 cm. *Photo Hirmer.*

64 Ivory. Transport of a relic. Sixth or seventh century. The Cathedral Treasury, Trier. Length 26·1 cm. Height 13·1 cm. *Photo Schmitt-Glassner.*

65 Silk from the tomb of Charlemagne, Aachen. The silk was probably introduced into the tomb when it was opened in the year 1000 by Otto III. Height 136 cm. Total width 162 cm. *Photo former Schlossmuseum, Berlin.*

66 Silk. The shroud of St Chaffre, Monastier, Haute Loire. Tenth or early eleventh century. Height 52·5 cm. Width 62·5 cm. *Photo Archives photographiques.*

67 Silk with riders in medallions. The Treasury of St Servais, Maastricht. Eighth century. Height 24·3 cm. Width 13·5 cm. *Photo Byzantine Exhibition, 1958 (No. 101).*

68 Ivory casket. Eleventh century. Palazzo Venezia, Rome. The casket has been assigned to various places by different authorities; it is certainly a provincial work. Height 12 cm. Length 16·5 cm. Width 11·5 cm. *Photo Hirmer.*

69 Ivory casket. The Veroli casket. Detail of front. Eleventh century. The Victoria and Albert Museum, London. Total length 40·5 cm. Height 11·5 cm. *Museum photo.*

70 Ivory casket. Front, end top. Eleventh century. Troyes Cathedral. The designs on the ends reproduce a Chinese motif, probably conveyed by means of a textile. *Photo Hirmer.*

71 Mosaic in a chamber of the Palace of Roger II, Palermo. Twelfth century. *Photo Alinari.*

72, 73 Mosaics of the Great Mosque, Damascus. 715. Palace with the rivers of paradise below; view of a hill-town. *Photos de Lorey.*

74 Mosaic of an Archangel, on the vault before the apse, Church of Haghia Sophia, Constantinople. Third quarter of the ninth century. *Photo Byzantine Institute of America.*

75 Mosaic: the Annunciation. *c.* 1100. Daphni, near Athens. *Photo Powell.*

76 Enamels from the crown of Constantine Monomachos (1042–1055). The National Museum, Budapest. *Museum photo.*

77 Ivory triptych: the Crucifixion and Saints. *c.* 988. The British Museum. Height 27·5 cm. Width central leaf 16·3 cm. *Photo Hirmer.*

78 Ivory triptych. The Deesis above, and Saints below and on the wings. Late tenth century. It is known as the Harbaville triptych. The Louvre Museum, Paris. *Photo Hirmer.*

79 Reliquary for a fragment of the True Cross, in gold and enamel. *c.* 960. Treasury of the cathedral at Limburg on the Lahn. Height 48 cm. Width 35 cm. *Photo Hirmer.*

80 Chalice of onyx, on gold base, with border of cloisonné enamels. Eleventh century. Treasury of St. Mark's, Venice. Height almost 25 cm. *Photo Böhm.*

81 Paten of silver, with the Crucifixion at the centre. Eleventh century. Treasury of the cathedral of Halberstadt. Diameter 38·8 cm. *Treasury photo.*

82 Mosaic in the south gallery, Haghia Sophia, Constantinople. Christ between the Empress Zoe and the Emperor Constantine Monomachos. Figures *c.* 1028; Constantine's portrait *c.* 1042. Height 2·44 m. Width 2·40 m.

83 Mosaic in the south gallery, Haghia Sophia, Constantinople. The Virgin and Child between the Emperor John II Comnenus and the Empress Irene. *c.* 1118. Height 2·47 m. Width 4·45 m. *Photo Hirmer.*

84 Icon. Our Lady of Vladimir. Probably painted in Constantinople about 1130. The Tretiakov Gallery, Moscow. Height 105 cm. Width 68·5 cm. The type is that known as 'Our Lady of Tenderness'. *Museum photo.*

85 Wall painting in the apse of the Church of Haghia Sophia, Ochrid. *c.* 1050. Nikopea type. *Photo Department of Ancient Monuments of Macedonia.*

86 Icon in the Museum of Fine Arts, Moscow. Fourteenth century. The type is that of the Hodegetria. *Museum photo.*

87 Wall painting. Detail of the Nativity. Nerez, near Skopolje, Macedonia. 1164. *Photo Department of Ancient Monuments, Macedonia.*

88 Wall painting. Detail of the Annunciation; the Virgin. Mileševa. *c.* 1235. *Photo Department of Ancient Monuments, Serbia.*

89 Wall painting. Detail of the Nativity; two shepherds. Sopoćani. *c.* 1260. *Photo Department of Ancient Monuments, Serbia.*

90 Mosaic: the Deesis. In the south gallery of Haghia Sophia, Constantinople. Probably late twelfth century. Width 4·08 m. *Photo Hirmer.*

91 Mosaic: the Numbering of the People. Kariye Camii, Constantinople. *c.* 1310. *Photo Powell.*

92 Portraits of a Prince and Princess of the Palaeologue family, from the Lincoln College Typicon, f. 6. *c.* 1400. Height 25 cm. Width 18 cm. Miniature. *Photo Bodleian Library.*

93 The Emperor Nicephorus Botiniates and his principal officers, with two allegorical figures above. *c.* 1078. Bibliothèque Nationale, Paris. Coislin. 79, f. 2. Height 41·5 cm. Width 3·5 cm. *Library photo.*

94 Miniature. The High Admiral Apocaucos. *c.* 1342. From a copy of Hippocrates in the Bibliothèque Nationale, Paris. Gr. 2144, f. 11. Height 41·5 cm. Width 35 cm.

95 Mosaic. Portrait of Theodore Metochites, presenting a model of the church, now known as Kariye Camii, to Christ. In Kariye Camii, Constantinople. *c.* 1310. *Photo Powell.*

Index